Defending the History of Economic Thought

Defending the History of Economic Thought

Steven Kates

School of Economics, Finance and Marketing, RMIT University, Melbourne, Australia

Edward Elgar

Cheltenham, UK • Northampton, MA, USA

Published by
Edward Elgar Publishing Limited
The Lypiatts
15 Lansdown Road
Cheltenham
Glos GL50 2JA
UK

Edward Elgar Publishing, Inc.
William Pratt House
9 Dewey Court
Northampton
Massachusetts 01060
USA

A catalogue record for this book
is available from the British Library

Library of Congress Control Number: 2013931629

This book is available electronically in the ElgarOnline.com
Economics Subject Collection, E-ISBN 978 1 78254 781 5

ISBN 978 1 84844 820 9

Typeset by Columns Design XML Ltd, Reading
Printed and bound in Great Britain by T.J. International Ltd, Padstow

Contents

Preface

> One should no more study modern price theory without knowing Adam Smith than one should read Adam Smith without having learned modern price theory.
>
> (Mark Blaug)

This book is about the importance of the study of the history of economic thought to the practice of economics. There is often discussion on why it is important for economists to have individually studied HET, a belief I entirely share. It is important for an economist to have an understanding of the evolution of economic theory through historical time, an understanding of the controversies that surrounded the development of economic thought and a solid grasp of ideas that have been overlooked, forgotten or discarded. But there is more to it than the education of individual economists, the microeconomic side of HET let us say. There is also the macroeconomic side and the value to economics as a whole in having within the ranks of economists many who are versed in the economic theories of the past.

The history of economic thought is a necessary although poorly recognised ingredient in the study and practice of economics. Without a significant proportion of economists actively examining the economics of the past and bringing these older ideas into the conversation in the present, economics is a lesser subject and economic theory less penetrating and of less value.

This book was commenced following an attempt by the Australian Bureau of Statistics to classify the history of economic thought out of existence by relocating its study into a new grouping, "History, Archaeology, Religion and Philosophy", a newly-devised makeshift catch-all category. The transfer would have meant that research into the history of economic thought would no longer have been considered research into economics itself, which would, in turn, have meant the virtual disappearance of research into HET within departments of economics. It would not have ended the study of the history of economics but as small as the cohort of specialists already was, it would have become smaller still.

But it was not until 2011, when the European Research Council also considered removing the history of economic thought from within the economics division, that I decided to bring this book to completion. The Australian experience turned out to have been not a one-off episode but a reflection of deeper currents which have by no means subsided.

Having been personally involved in helping to reverse both the Australian and European attempts at reclassification, I have given a great deal of thought to the role and significance of the history of economic thought as an essential part of economics. These considerations have led to a deeper appreciation of why HET is a necessary component of economics. And this is not just about classification systems. Although many economists now ignore the history of economic thought and in some cases actually disdain its very existence, this book attempts to explain why the study of HET is not only a crucial element in the education of an economist but is also a necessary component of economic theory in and of itself.

The history of economics is not a sub-discipline of economics, it is economics. Economics is an amalgam of theories and techniques that can be used to make sense of the ways in which we provide for our material wellbeing. There are no end of economic problems and there are no end of ways to examine problems and devise solutions. Some of these ways are as modern as the present, others, most others, are an inheritance from the past, some from the distant past. Options worth consideration are sometimes found in the most recently published textbooks or embodied in the latest crop of journal articles. Others can only be found in books, tracts, pamphlets, articles and papers written years before. What the study of the history of economic thought does is bring all of these alternative perspectives into active consideration.

In putting this book together, which began with my researches related to the Australian Bureau of Statistics and then to the European Research Council, I have read an enormous amount of material. Lamentably, I cannot acknowledge each of the works that have gone into informing me during this research. But the fact of the matter is that there is an enormous amount of material – almost all of it directed at why individual economists should individually study the history of economic thought. The nature of the research and the presentations made to the ABS and ERC were aimed at demonstrating a different proposition, that the history of economic thought is a necessary and important part of the study of economics. It cannot be hived off somewhere else without serious damage. Studying the history of economic thought improves the development of economic theory and the practice of applied economics. The fact that this is so very little appreciated has made the writing of this book a necessity.

But while I have read much I would also like to acknowledge the assistance of a number of people. The first of these is my Australian colleague, Alex Millmow. We worked together to preserve the history of economics in Australia and the only conclusion I have is that he has missed a career in politics. His tireless and focused efforts to maintain the role of HET need to be recognised and I appreciated his partnership in achieving the outcome we did.

I am also grateful for the kind help and generous assistance of Cristina Marcuzzo, who, as President of the European Society for the History of Economic Thought, assisted us in Australia when the reclassification decision was being determined and again understood the nature of the threat when the European Research Council was considering the same change in Europe.

I would also like to thank E. Roy Weintraub and Steven Medema for their willingness to engage in this conversation, which has been important in clarifying the issues at stake. Having a different opinion on how to preserve the study of the history of economics is why we discuss and debate. I am grateful for the time they devoted to setting their views out so that they could be better understood and discussed. We may not agree on everything but these are honest disagreements.

I am also eternally grateful to my wife, Zuzanna. Books take time and patience and Susie has always had the extraordinary patience required that has allowed me the time to bring this and so much else to completion.

But finally, the book is dedicated to the memory of Mark Blaug (1927–2011), in my view the twentieth century's finest historian of economic thought. I learned more from him personally and from his written work than from anyone else I have had the pleasure of dealing with. His *Economic Theory in Retrospect*, the only book from my days as a student that I still have on my shelf (revised edition, 1968), set a standard for scholarship that I knew I could never hope to equal but also made me wish that I knew more about the history of economic thought, a major reason why I have had a continuing life-long interest in HET. No more can ever be asked of a teacher than that he should be an inspiration to his students. In finishing, let me quote these words from the preface to the first edition of his *Economic Theory in Retrospect*, which this book has tried to amplify and explain:

> In truth, one should no more study modern price theory without knowing Adam Smith than one should read Adam Smith without having learned modern price theory. There is a mutual interaction between past and present economic thinking for, whether we set it down in so many words or not, the history of economic thought is being rewritten every generation. (Blaug [1962] 1968: ix)

This was written in 1962. The most up-to-date theories of that time are now part of the history of economics, just as what we write today will also and inevitably become part of that same history. But in the same way that Mark Blaug has something of value to say to us today, so we will have something of value to say to the future, just as the past will continue to have something of value to say to us.

1. Preliminary thoughts

> The master economist must possess a rare *combination* of gifts. … He must be mathematician, *historian*, statesman and philosopher.
> (John Maynard Keynes, 1925: the first italics his, the second mine)

Is the only economics worth knowing the economics found in the latest texts and in journal articles no more than twenty years old? For many an economist the answer is an unambiguous yes. Almost all economics is now learned from the most recent editions of homogenised texts and reference to articles written more than a decade or two before are rare. Economics to most economists has no history worth knowing.

Economists once knew better. Every economist at one time learned the history of their own subject. Every economist once read from their forebears and learned their own modern economic theory in an environment that insisted upon an understanding of the economics of the past. Yet somehow and for some reason, the same economists who were brought up reading Adam Smith, David Ricardo, John Stuart Mill and Alfred Marshall, to cite only from the English tradition, commenced a change in the discipline so that almost no one now does the same.

It is an established view within the mainstream that there is nothing to be gained from having access to the historical tradition. Those within the profession who were themselves taught about the history of their subject have been complicit in the removal of HET from the syllabus and have all but pushed it into the attic of discarded relics. They have promoted the notion that the latest theories embody the only sets of ideas that need ever be entertained. Historical views, the soil from which our current ideas have grown, are not even seen as worth so much as a single semester of a student's time.

Instead students of economics are served a diet of pre-digested concepts whose historical origins only a small and diminishing proportion of economists now know. Other than in the most rudimentary ways, none of the debates that led to the acceptance of one set of theories rather than another is taught. Adam Smith wrote a revolutionary work of almost a thousand pages, a work that changed the direction of our entire culture and began a transformation of the world, yet few would know much more than that he wrote of an "invisible hand" as a metaphor for the market.

There was, it is understood, a marginal revolution during the latter decades of the nineteenth century. Marginal concepts are embedded at every stage of economic analysis, yet who would know what came before, who effected the change from what was then to what there is now, and how the nature of economic theory became different as a result.

Even an event as momentous as the Keynesian revolution is largely an unknown. Economists are taught of the existence of a "classical" theory and then told not to go there. Yet there was a theory of the cycle that had more than satisfied some of the greatest minds economics has ever produced and it had developed for over a century. It had been this very theory that was successfully applied in most of the world to end the Great Depression. Yet not one economist in a hundred could tell you what that theory of the cycle was or how or in what way Keynes changed economics.

Worse still, few would know why it matters. The value of discarded error is set at close to zero. Thinking about superseded ideas is seen as a waste of time better spent coming to grips with the latest statistical techniques and mathematical tools. What's worth knowing is bundled into the latest texts and the rest can be happily ignored with no loss to anyone. If any of it were worth knowing, we would know it already, to paraphrase an ancient economic parable.[1]

The present book is about why the history of economics is a necessary part of economics itself and why economists ought to learn it. Good economics requires a knowledge of the history of economic theory. Without embedding a historical understanding into a theoretical perspective, the results will be poorly framed and

---

[1] Along the lines of there cannot be a twenty dollar bill lying on the ground because if there were, someone would already have picked it up.

badly designed. Economists have always known this; such knowledge has always been embedded into both new theoretical directions and policy design.

Yet it is a form of knowledge that is being denied to new entrants to the field who are therefore made less capable of thinking about theory and understanding its nature. They are less able to employ theory in a creative way because they are taught economics as if it is comprised of a series of mechanical technical solutions to what are, in fact, some of the most intractable social problems human beings are ever forced to deal with. An appreciation of the organic nature of economic theory, an attempt to understand in different historical times and different social environments the actual circumstances of the surrounding economic questions in need of an answer, presents the study of economics in a very different light. This is, at its most basic, what studying the history of economic thought allows economists to do. It reminds economists that economics is a social science and not physics.

Presented thus, the history of economics is seen in a utilitarian way, as an input into good economic practice. And so it is. But none of this is to deny the pleasures of studying the history of economics because of its intrinsic interest. The history of economic thought is also part of the history and philosophy of science. It satisfies the needs for philosophical and social understanding. It is an area worth studying just for the pure pleasure of knowledge for its own sake.

This, too, is important to understand. It is important to appreciate that economics, like any other science, say chemistry, astronomy, evolutionary theory or whatever, has an interest for the non-specialist who can enjoy and learn from a study of the development of economic theory and its historical practice. There are many fascinating details to be discovered in showing how the answers found in our textbooks today were formed through the interplay of different personalities at different moments in the past. Some of the great economic debates of bygone eras have been of major importance in setting the political agenda in different periods of time.

Beyond this, the history of economics provides a depth of understanding to political and social issues. It sheds light on many historical events that cannot be understood without simultaneously understanding the economic considerations that were being entertained at the same time. Economic theory has played its own independent role in the unfolding of the social and political history of the world. Without an understanding of the contrasting theoretical perspectives, the events themselves are difficult if not actually impossible to understand.

All this is fascinating stuff, both for the non-specialist and for economists themselves. But that is not why economists must know the history of their subject. What matters is not that it is interesting but that it provides a depth and balance to their own theoretical understanding of the world. These cannot be gained in any other way except through the study of the development of economic thought.

The history of economic thought provides vital case studies. A theory comes into existence because it occurred to some particular economist of the past that some particular way of examining the world would provide the answer to some particular economic question. The tools of the economics trade were discovered one by one in just this kind of way. It is possible, as we regularly do, to remove these theories from their original settings and place them within the artificial hothouse atmosphere of the economics text. But in so doing, the theory has been removed from the background in which it was devised and risks becoming an arid conjecture, isolated from its surrounding context. It is a lifeless artefact, a conclusion supported by the thousands of economic students who often fail to see the relevance of the theories they are made to absorb.

It took a hundred years, from the time of Adam Smith until the mid-1870s, for marginal utility theory to find its way into the conscious processes of economic thought. That same theory can be taught in an afternoon or perhaps two at most. A bit of the diamond–water paradox, an issue raised by Adam Smith right at the start, might raise some weak appreciation of the ways in which the various considerations unfolded. But when push comes to shove, there is very little history taught in explaining marginal utility and the entire theory becomes little more than yet another gadget in a series of micro tools used to explain the world.

In a classroom setting, that might be all that can be done. But if the aim is to achieve a rounded education for an economist, to leave things there would be pitifully inadequate. Economists, especially if they see economics as a sub-branch of mathematics, might find it difficult to understand the value to themselves in coming to grips with the evolution of theoretical concepts. There might be little if any appreciation of Bentham and the utilitarian school or what an understanding of past work may say to economists in the present day. Jevons, Menger and Walras may never mean much to some healthy proportion of the economists made to endure this historical instruction. They may see no significance in the shift in economics from its classical *social* origins to the view of economics as the study of *atomistic individuals* who are seen to be looking after their own interests all on their own. But at the end of the day, something of value is learned. And what is learned is what the theory actually meant when it was fresh in the world and new. It puts a different perspective on the theory that is being drummed into students at every stage of their economic education. And the economist-in-training can recognise the origins of the tradition out of which the knowledge put to use has grown.

Economists who understand this kind of history are different. They have broader knowledge, their understanding is deeper. They have a facility in the use of this area of economic thought that brings to life the various economic questions to which this part of theory is applied. It connects economic theory to broader social questions. It gives economic theory a sense of depth that is otherwise absent. It turns a technician into an economist. It adds interest where there was previously little. It brings colour to what had until then been grey. It adds insights not found in a modern text. It brings economics to life where before it was dead.

Compare an economist who, *ceteris paribus*, understands the origins and evolution of marginal utility theory with one who does not. Can it realistically be said that they are in any sense equal? Is it not obvious that the extra depth and detail provided by bringing the history to the subject has changed the way the world is seen and understood? This is not just history for history's sake. It is not just learning something with no application. It is providing a dynamic understanding that makes someone a better economist, one who will better understand the issues that need to be dealt with than one who has not taken on the same kind of historical study.

But it is more than just the individual economist who is more knowledgeable. It is the profession itself, the entire body of economists, who have that deeper, broader understanding. Ideas that had been considered in the past are introduced into the conversation. Different ways of looking at issues are discussed. The notion that the latest answers are always the best answers is implicitly, if not explicitly, rejected.

WHO THIS BOOK IS FOR

The Economics Profession in General

This book is, firstly, for those who may not even know that they ought to know something about the history of economics. I start with the economics profession in general. It is now a commonly held belief amongst economists that they do not truly benefit from knowing the history of their subject. Other than as an archipelago of scattered and unrelated just-so stories, there is little appreciation of the wealth of frameworks, concepts and ideas that lie buried in the almost entirely ignored history of their subject, nor is there a belief that they ought to know more than they do. In getting on with what they consider the real work of economics, there is no need to investigate what are seen as primitive early attempts to make sense of how economies worked.

Amongst economists of even the recent past, many if not most would have studied the history of the subject. Amongst such economists, there was a deeper knowledge of the history of their subject that influenced and shaped their ability to undertake studies in economics. It provided an ever-present background that affected their work without anyone much bothering to take note of how and where this historical understanding had seeped into their publications and ideas.

And yet it was this same cohort of economists who were responsible for allowing HET to disappear from the core curriculum. While the subject became more quantitative, those who had the historical knowledge actively limited the availability of such knowledge to the generations that have followed behind.

The book is therefore in the first instance an appeal to economists generally, and in particular to those who are in a position to influence such decisions, to return the study of the history of economic thought to the economics curriculum. Some of the great economists of the past, steeped in the mathematical tradition, if revealed preference is anything to go by understood the value of studying and teaching HET. Just to restrict myself to names beginning with "S", there were Samuelson, Stigler and Schumpeter, each of whom devoted time and thought to examining the economic theories of the past. These investigations inevitably shaped the way they understood economic issues. Their interest was not in the sociology of knowledge. Their interest was in understanding how economies worked. Their studies of economists of the past were written for economists of their own time as a means of explaining the approaches adopted in earlier days and to make sense of the blur of economic events.

This is a tradition that has been closed off in large parts of the academic world and there is only one group that can open this study up again. Only those who teach economics and set the curriculum can make this change. In the final analysis this book is aimed at those who are able to make these changes in the curriculum.

Students of Economics

The second group to whom this book is addressed are the next generation of economists who have not had the opportunity to study HET. Economics has in many ways become more mathematically inclined, and may even be attracting a different kind of mentality into its orbit in comparison with days past. This next generation and the ones to follow may by nature have little interest in possessing an understanding of the historical development of their science and may have no appreciation that these old discarded ideas may strike a spark in their own minds about the very subject matter of their own areas of research. Thus in many ways this book is addressed to economists who have never had the opportunity to look into the way in which their science formed, and more importantly, have no ready access to the wealth of ideas, concepts and theories that were once the central substance of their field of knowledge. Indeed, it is not just what was known, but also the form in which such past knowledge was known, the different ways of thinking about these issues, that has been lost.

Economics is more than a set of equations. It has since its first days been at the centre of political controversies of the most astonishingly intense kind. It is not an exaggeration to say that the world almost annihilated itself over the economic question posed by Karl Marx and then taken up by the Marxist regimes. The Cold War was about the organisation of economies, about who should own the means of production, individuals or the state. On the two sides of the iron curtain were ranged nuclear weapons that threatened the entire population of the earth while the economic issues of public versus private ownership were worked through. This is only the most extreme example of the role that economic issues have played in the social and political world that surrounds us all.

Economics is a social science. It has always tapped into the roots of the societies in which theories were developed. For those who see economics only as the solution to a set of equations, the more societal aspects of economics may be of limited interest. But for others who take an interest in broader and deeper social questions, one of the most useful points of entry is through the history of economics and the discussion of the development of theory against the background of the times in which different theories rose to prominence. Economists who are unaware that there are such ways of engaging with economics are deprived of the benefits that can only come from having had the experience of learning the history of their own subject.

To such economists and students of economics this book has been addressed. It is to let you know that if you are an economist and you have not studied the history of economic thought, that your own education as an economist has not been as full as it could have been or ought to have been. It is possible, perhaps even likely, that there is only the most minimal appreciation that something is missing in your own expertise. But think of this. You will never have been in contact with the great ideas of the past nor have you looked at the ways in which their ideas were originally expressed. If you have not looked into, as a minimum, Adam Smith's *Wealth of Nations*, David Ricardo's *Principles of Political Economy and Taxation*, John Stuart Mill's *Principles of Political Economy*, Karl Marx's *Capital*, Stanley Jevons's *Theory of Political Economy*, Alfred Marshall's *Principles of Economics* and John Maynard Keynes's *General Theory of Employment, Interest and Money*, then you have deprived yourself of some of the greatest writings on economics that there have ever been. And if you do not know who each and every one of these writers is, then your education as an economist has fallen well short of the mark for someone aspiring to be a genuine scholar.

If you wish to be an economist, you should seek to know more about the economic theories of the past. You should not just accept that you will go through life without knowing who the great names in economics are and what their ideas were. You should not accept that you will have no idea where the theories that populate your texts began their life or how they developed. But most importantly, you should not accept that your knowledge base will remain as limited as is the necessary case if all you have ever learned are the pre-digested views found in economics texts and the most recent contributions to economic debates that have gone on for hundreds of years.

An economics PhD thesis normally begins with a literature search that asks the candidate to go back through the development of the ideas of that part of economic theory to which the original contribution will be made. There is an explicit understanding that knowledge in depth is dependent on having the detailed background that provides a framework and context for the work that will be undertaken. This is explicit recognition that to add to the accumulated understanding in a subject area there is a prior need to have worked through the historical journey that had led up to the way in which the subject is conceived at the present time. Undertaking a doctorate is, of course, a unique experience in the training of an economist. But the lesson that ought to be drawn from this requirement is that the way in which our present understanding has developed through the evolution of past ideas is an essential element in having a full and detailed comprehension of those ideas as they presently exist.

The depth of understanding required as a doctoral candidate is greater than the requirements in understanding economic theory in general, but the principle is the same and the level of depth that should be developed should not be seen to be all that different. The economic theory of the past is the rudder that has guided the development of thought to its present mooring. You cannot fully understand the theory as it is presented in its most recent version without the orientation provided by the historical development of the relevant ideas. There is always something of significance left out as theory is moulded and shaped to fit into its textbook frame. And you don't know what it is until you look into it yourself and mix your own knowledge and way of thinking with the ideas that shaped earlier generations of economists, and which over time and through the pressure of events and personalities developed into economic theory as it is found today.

Communicating economic ideas

And the matter even for economics students does not end there. Most of the work economists do requires an ability to communicate with those with no economics training. Going back to the origins of economics takes one to a time before there was a professional class of economists and to discussions which, at this earliest stage, were discussions between interested individuals who were looking at economies not that different from our own with problems not that different from our own. Different institutional settings, perhaps, and different communal beliefs, but the core issues that were alive then are the ones alive today, and this will be true at any time, past, present, or in the future. Listening in on these earlier conversations between economists about how economies were structured and how policy should be designed provides a backdrop against which our own modern theories can be measured.

Economists need the ability to speak a language of economics for the non-economist. To enter a conversation on economic matters with those with neither economic training nor the jargon of economic theory at hand, to discuss economic issues with those who wish to understand the point being made in a language they can follow requires a different kind of training from the ability to speak to someone else who has studied economic theory. It requires an ability to explain in words and concepts ideas that are often embedded within a theoretical structure that is incomprehensible to someone without the same background knowledge and expertise. Translating the results of an equation into words is an important skill that the study of the history of economic thought helps to develop.

And for the student of economics, amongst the most important and valuable reasons for studying the theories of a bygone period is that students can learn from what these supposedly obsolete economists once said and wrote. There are perspectives on issues that were expressed in the past that may have failed to gain mainstream acceptance but that nevertheless are worth considering and testing against one's own ways of thinking about issues. It is even possible that there are ways of thinking about economic issues that had not previously been encountered that might prove to be unexpectedly convincing. Economics is not physics, where past ways of thinking about theoretical issues will never return and if they did would only return in a completely different way. With economics earlier ideas were based on observations similar to those made in the present. The generalisations that were made then, that is, the theories that were formulated to explain events, may have more explanatory power than one might have expected. This is the risk and the benefit of examining older theories. There is the potential to disturb one's existing approach to economic issues, and at the very least, if this is not the case, the possibility of deepening the views one already holds as they are tested against the views of an earlier time.

Where there is a profound certainty that these earlier economists were wrong in what they had written, the ability to explain just what is wrong with their superseded ways of thinking is a valuable form of training in itself. Putting oneself into another's shoes and viewing matters from other perspectives in relation to some controversy of the time helps develop one's own perspective and brings additional dimensions to one's own ways of thinking. Being able to explain – even to oneself – the reasoning behind someone else's arguments, to understand why it had been a satisfying way of understanding some issue, develops critical abilities within an economic context, and is as effective a way as any for improving one's abilities as an economist. Whatever "errors" they may have made, their views will not be superficial but will consist of deeply considered economic ideas that had been accepted by their contemporaries and whose comprehension can provide considerable insight even now.

In sum, for a student of economics to delve into the history of their subject deepens their understanding of the theories they use, allows them to be tested against a different framework of analysis and opens the possibility of finding genuine insights into the way the economy works. In addition, working through such theories develops the ability to explain economics to those without an economics background, the capacity to articulate one's perspectives in a convincing way and to sharpen one's own analytical abilities. One more course in mathematical technique will provide fewer long-term benefits. This is the case even if one's future aim is an academic career. It is all the more so if one's career aspiration is to work in policy or in any other environment in which communication with others of diverse backgrounds is expected. A widening perspective and a deeper understanding of economic theory can never go amiss. The marginal benefit will in almost every instance far exceed the marginal cost. Real education will be the result.

Employers of Economists

It is also the employers of economists who should be interested in economists with an understanding of the history of economic theory. These are the people who are looking to provide jobs to economics graduates and, indeed, to economists at every level. They are therefore in a very powerful position to determine what students should study, and if they themselves understand what they ought to be looking for in an economically trained employee, they will certainly hope to have employees with a knowledge of the history of their subject.

Quite clearly it would be a very rare job that required anyone to understand the history of economics per se. No job – not in the public sector nor in the private – would ever likely have such a requirement. But what almost all such jobs do have is a requirement for an employee to exhibit the skills that having a background in the history of economic theory provides.

What are employers looking for? They are looking for employees who are not only capable of understanding situations from a variety of perspectives but who are also able to provide articulate non-technical explanations of their points of view. Economists in a workplace setting must be able to explain their conclusions and often must explain their reasoning as well. For an employer of economists, that must be an essential requirement. Seldom will an economist be asked to reach a conclusion and then act on it without first discussing with someone else either the reasoning behind their recommendations or the actions to be taken. A study of the history of economics is an indication that this kind of ability is present in an employee.

An employer will prefer to employ economists who have a range of ideas and who have the potential to look at various questions from a number of alternative perspectives. Someone who has studied the history of economics has demonstrated at least some capacity of this kind.

An employer will prefer employees who have a wider field of vision in looking into issues, who have at their command different ways of looking at a problem and who have made an effort during their studies to engage with ideas somewhat alien to their own normal perspective. They will normally hope to have in their employees the ability to identify an appropriate framework with which to confront a problem. They will therefore find it beneficial to have employees with the wider perspective that studying the history of economics provides.

If you cannot have such knowledge embodied in any prospective employee, then it is unavailable. But if some students do study HET and others do not, then it can become a point of discrimination between candidates. It is here that the preferences of employers can become decisive. If employers show a preference for candidates who have some understanding of HET, and recognise the depth and breadth that such additional knowledge can provide in a work environment, then it will become a stimulus for students to be taught such courses.

The fact of the matter is that most economists will not end up in a graduate school nor will they end up teaching the subject. They will be very unlikely to do the kinds of research that would justify that one additional course in mathematics or statistics that might replace a course in HET. Most economists when they embark on their careers are undertaking a very different kind of work far away from a university setting. Professional economists in the corporate world or in government will be doing the kinds of analysis that lends itself to a more historical and analytical approach. The kinds of disciplines that the training in HET provides develops precisely the kinds of skills that are frequently the most useful in a non-academic workplace setting.

But even in an academic setting, there are many who value the history of economics as an integral part of the training of a rounded economist. Here, too, it can make a difference if knowledge of the history of economic thought becomes a criterion for selection and its absence a negative feature. A student who has successfully completed work in the history of economics has knowledge that is useful in understanding theory but which is unavailable to colleagues who have not. They are less narrow and have a greater appreciation of the sweep of economic ideas over time. They are more comfortable in dealing with older texts, which they will more likely hold in higher regard. They will know there are sources of insight in books and articles of a previous period, and if their training has been appropriate, will be able to use such resources to further their own research.

General Interest

Finally, there are individuals who are just interested in economics and would like to have a greater knowledge of the subject. One could take an introductory course in micro/macro which would leave a student with the incomplete knowledge that any such course must leave them with. Or as an alternative, in the same way as one might attempt to learn about physics or chemistry by reading about the development of the subject areas across time, so one might learn about economics through studying its history. While it would not prepare someone for work as a professional economist, it would introduce them to the subject in just the right sort of way. That is, they would learn the subject by reading about the development of the various theories found in our texts, within the context of the times in which they entered the canon and with the surrounding debates and economic circumstances to provide a framework to assist in making sense of the theoretical conclusions.

In fact, a history of economics course that was designed for students who had not previously studied economics may well be far preferable as a means of grasping the various associated ideas than an introductory course in economic principles. Marginal utility taught against the framework of the classical theory of value, or macroeconomics taught as a response to the Great Depression, would almost certainly provide a more useful way of thinking about economic questions than would a poorly grasped course in pure theory. In neither case would the student at the end of such a course be able to say they have a genuine understanding of economic principles, but the student doing the history of economics would not expect to, and would be less likely to succumb to the pitfalls of a little knowledge being a dangerous thing; rather they would have some idea of the complexity of the problems involved and the difficulty economic theory has in making coherent sense of the world.

FINAL COMMENT

It is nothing short of remarkable that economists no longer study the history of their subject, that they have only the most superficial appreciation of what came before. There are reasons for this. There is a lot to learn and there are trade-offs involved in how time is spent. The more that economics has become mathematicised, the less time that can apparently be devoted to what appears to many within the profession as a passenger in the study of theory and applied technique.

Yet as Keynes wrote, an economist "must possess a rare *combination* of gifts … must be mathematician, historian, statesman and philosopher". Or as Alfred Marshall – who famously put the maths into the appendices – wrote on the very first page of his *Principles*, "economics is a study of mankind in the ordinary business of life". Economics is a study that requires an understanding of individuals within their historical, social and institutional settings. It is an attempt to reply to questions asked by the world itself which, if they can be answered properly, will add to the wealth and wellbeing of the entire human race. Economics has become very mathematical. But a mathematical answer to an economic question is seldom any answer at all unless it can be put into words and the conclusions explained in terms of historical circumstance. The history of economic thought is itself a form of technique, partly assisting its students in how to comprehend what others have said and partly in explaining economic concepts and conclusions in ways that others can follow.

But more importantly still, studying the history of economics makes someone a better economist. That is why it should be studied. That is what this book is designed to explain.

2. Why study the history of economic thought

> He who limits himself to knowing only the epoch in which he lives, even if it enjoys a marked superiority over its predecessors, exposes himself to the danger of partaking of all its superstitions; for each generation has its own, and it would be exceedingly dangerous to fancy oneself so close to the ultimate limits of reason that one no longer had to fear these prejudices.
>
> (Marquis de Condorcet; quoted by Manuel, 1962: 66)

Economists by and large believe they do not need to know the history of their subject to be good economists. They seem to believe that somehow they have been bequeathed a set of theories, tools and concepts that may be found in any of a vast number of texts, and that these theories, tools and concepts are all that is needed to undertake any task with which an economist might be presented. They do not need to know how the theory developed, what it was that the most recent theories replaced, what debates went on at the time, nor any of the subsequent controversies that may have surrounded those theories after they had been formulated and entered the canon. Nor do they seem to believe that it would be preferable to be instructed in those theories through the writings of the individual economists who first introduced those ideas into economic discourse. None of that is seen to be necessary in order to become as good an economist as it is possible to be.

No one puts it quite like that. Most economists have some smattering of historical knowledge, which gives them a sense that they do know something of their subject's past. They all know something about Adam Smith and John Maynard Keynes. They are likely to have heard about mercantilism and Say's Law. There is an awareness of the "marginal revolution". But all of this is mere background. To the extent any of this is known at all, it is known in only the most hazy way.

An economist is not likely to have much of an understanding of history of any kind. History generally is largely disdained. In a subject without the possibility of repeatable experiments, there is still very little effort made to look into the past to understand what happened at different moments in time and to make sense of which policies work and which do not. There is little effort to use historical events to examine theories and test propositions. As the most egregious example, few economists have made an effort to understand even the Great Depression, what were its causes and what steps were taken to bring it to an end. And what is true of what might have been the single most important episode in the history of economics is still more true of other periods and events. Economists tend not to think in historical terms, neither about events nor about the development of their own subject. History, to the extent that there is any history, is merely a time series embedded within a set of data. It is not the actual specific contingent events that are the constituent elements of the past that are ever deeply understood by a practising economist.

Thus, economics becomes the latest textbook theories supplemented by the most recent articles in the most important journals. The closest neighbouring subject areas are seen to be amongst the hardest of the natural sciences. In particular, it is classical physics that comes closest to representing the economist's ideal. There are forces and there are theories that describe the various consequences of movement of those forces. There is no purpose in going over the way in which those theories were derived. They are what they are, and that is it.

But theories of the physical universe are not written by atoms about atoms. There is no theory in classical physics that argues that the objects of their studies have changed over the course of time so that what was once true is now less true and might eventually become untrue merely through the passage of time as a result of the unfolding of the universe. Physical theories are timeless. A discovery takes the subject to a higher plane but doesn't affect any of the elements about which theories are written, nor are those elements ever expected to change.

In physics, therefore, as in the other hard physical sciences, there is nothing in particular that can be learned about the contemporary state of the subject from its history. Kepler's laws, once discovered, remain true for all time, and knowledge of what Kepler did or when he did it and under what circumstances he made his discoveries have no relevance to the validity of the theories themselves. One is not a better physicist for knowing the history of physics.

This can never be the case in the social sciences. The social sciences are theories made by humans about various aspects of the human condition. The circumstances of a theory's birth are of critical importance in understanding the theory and the answers it is supposed to provide. Their origins provide the ideal case study that can help someone make sense of the theory and understand not just what it is trying to explain but also its limitations.

This may superficially seem to contradict the central thesis that the ideas of the past have relevance for today. But the point here is that it is the present ideas that may be the ones that have lost their relevance. Theories and technique may enter into the canon at some particular moment and thereafter persist even where the circumstances of the world make such theories less relevant or even no longer relevant. As Paul Samuelson very perceptively noted:

> Finally, and perhaps most important from the long-run standpoint, the Keynesian analysis has begun to filter down into the elementary textbooks; and as everybody knows once an idea gets into these, how-ever bad it may be, it becomes practically immortal. (Samuelson, 1948: 189)

A theory that looks at issues in one way may by its very nature exclude aspects important to a more rounded and comprehensive understanding of economic relations. Being taught theory as truth rather than as an evolved set of provisional conclusions which may illuminate some aspects of economic life while obscuring others changes the way economists look at their theories. Teaching theory as settled conclusions breeds an unwarranted complacency. It shuts out alternative ways of thinking.

To return to an example already referred to: mainstream theory, with the marginal revolution, moved to an individualistic approach in its thinking about human action. Every person is sovereign, decision-makers are to be taken individually, on their own. This leaves the social nature of human beings and their interactions outside economists' thinking about economic questions. Something is gained by looking at economic relations in this way, but something is also lost. An economist who takes the theory as found is unaware of the debates that went on at the time, the different perspectives that were brought to the marginal revolution, the forms of understanding that are ignored. Recognising any and all of this should make an economist more wary of taking textbook theory as a settled set of conclusions, applicable without modification. The history of theory is a form of user's guide to its application.

There is too little appreciation in the way that economics is taught and learned that the individual components that make up economies – the actual people living in those economies, their value systems, skills base, their aims and ambitions – have an effect on the ways economies unfold. They present limits to an economy's potential. An economist can argue that individuals will choose those options in which the flow of benefits relative to the flow of costs reaches a maximum. And that is possibly true as far as it goes. But if we are comparing, say, a member of the Amish community with a merchant banker, to argue that they will choose the best option for themselves is near enough empty as a means of understanding what they will do or the direction in which events might proceed. It is either a tautology or, even worse, a form of throwing sand in one's own eyes; it may well be an approach that gives economists the belief that something has been understood, when in fact they may have understood very little at all.

That there are other ways of looking at things is one of the most useful lessons we learn from studying the history of economics. It is, as Condorcet states, a dangerous delusion to believe that we are "so close to the ultimate limits of reason" that we no longer have to fear that we are subject to the prejudices and superstitions of our own times which, being our own prejudices and superstitions, are almost impossible to detect. Studying HET takes us out of our own time and place. It takes us into different modes of thinking. It makes us re-examine things we take for granted; it makes us consider, however briefly, those unstated assumptions we build into our thoughts without necessarily even being aware they are there.

Even the currently fashionable notion that the history of economics is of next to no value to an economist in doing economics, even that is a relatively modern belief that only really began to take on a life of its own in the 1970s. But it is not a belief that was shared by earlier generations of economists who took meticulous care in learning and teaching the history of their subject. Were they so completely wrong? Is studying HET equivalent to learning

Greek and Latin, of little practical use in the modern world, but whose absence of value was only finally recognised once the practice came to an end? Or did studying the history of the subject provide a subtlety and depth to the economics of the past which remain invisible to ourselves because we no longer make the effort to understand what those earlier economists had written?

WHAT ECONOMICS IS – WHAT ECONOMISTS DO

Economics is a policy science. Its role is not just to develop a set of abstract theoretical tools but is for the most part an attempt to provide a workable understanding of the nature and structure of the economy with the aim of framing economic policies. The majority of those with economics degrees will ultimately make their way in the world by applying the tools of the trade they have learned in an attempt to resolve real-world social puzzles. The role of HET should not therefore be narrowly framed in terms of economics as an academic study whose value is restricted only to academic pursuits, but should be conceived more broadly, to explicitly recognise the value of studying the history of economics as a means to learn and apply economic theory.

The issues that will be discussed in defence of HET are grouped under a number of general headings, but there is really only a single purpose: to demonstrate that a knowledge of the history of the relevant economic theories provides added and useful depth to whatever theoretical or empirical studies are being made. And the added depth is both a personal attribute of individual economists and part of the overall fabric of the study of economics.

Of course it is possible to undertake an economic investigation without any knowledge whatsoever of the history of the relevant theory. It is clear enough that this is what occurs on a daily basis across the vast expanse of economics. It is also clear enough that there are trade-offs in time and effort involved in determining just which forms of knowledge one should gather and apply to the issue under review. But what should also be clear is that a better understanding of the history of the theory being studied or applied adds to the weight of useful knowledge brought to bear on some question. The remainder of this chapter will attempt to demonstrate just how much this is the case and will be aimed at demonstrating the ways in which the history of economic thought is able to add to the education of an economist, the depth of their analyses and the conclusions they reach by providing economists with:

- a contrast between their own theories and the theories of their predecessors
- a perspective on existing theory that provides orientation for its future development
- a conversation with the economists of the past on contemporary questions
- a storehouse of theoretical approaches for dealing with economic issues
- a means of deepening their own understanding of contemporary theory
- a means of deepening their own ability to handle theoretical questions
- a literary approach to dealing with economic issues different from but as valid as mathematical and statistical approaches
- a means for training applied economists
- an alternative pathway for teaching economic theory and its application.

None of this is to deny that studying the history of economics simply for the academic rewards that such knowledge provides is in itself often justification enough. There are indeed many such rewards and many who focus on the history of economic thought do so because of the intrinsic interest of the subject. The history of economic thought is a valuable study in its own right, quite apart from any practical role it might play in deepening the work of an economist in studying economic issues. But what will be argued below is that the study of the history of theory also provides a foundation for both economic research and applied economics that is ignored in ways that threaten to limit the value of economics and deplete the analytical ability of economists. Each of these issues is discussed only in brief since far more could be said about each. But the larger point, that an economist without a background in the history of the subject is less well equipped – even in dealing with straightforward economic questions – than one who does have such knowledge, is the central contention of the remainder of this chapter and of the book as a whole.

A CONTRAST WITH THE THEORIES OF ONE'S PREDECESSORS

Economists have almost from the start looked to earlier times to find contrasting approaches to dealing with economic questions as a means to highlight what is novel in their own.

Adam Smith in *The Wealth of Nations* contrasted his view of the conditions under which economies would best perform with the mercantilist doctrines of his predecessors. It was the belief that wealth consists of gold and silver and not in the productions of a nation that was, according to Smith, the supreme error of both concept and policy.[1] These were, he argued, the views of his contemporaries, but in rooting out this error he went into the past. He looked firstly at the views he attributed to John Locke, who had written a century before himself. (And feel free to skip the next four quotes from Smith. Alas reading eighteenth-century prose does require a skill most economists no longer have (which is part of the problem).)

> Mr. Locke remarks a distinction between money and other movable goods. All other movable goods, he says, are of so consumable a nature that the wealth which consists in them cannot be much depended on, and a nation which abounds in them one year may, without any exportation, but merely their own waste and extravagance, be in great want of them the next. Money, on the contrary, is a steady friend, which, though it may travel about from hand to hand, yet if it can be kept from going out of the country, is not very liable to be wasted and consumed. Gold and silver, therefore, are, according to him, the most solid and substantial part of the movable wealth of a nation, and to multiply those metals ought, he thinks, upon that account, to be the great object of its political œconomy. (Smith [1776] 1976: 451)

Smith continues by noting how these views became generally accepted within nations that engaged in international trade. It is one thing, they had argued, if trade did not occur, but quite another where it did:

---

[1] It is, moreover, probable that there will be scholars who will read this sentence and see in it some pathetic solecism. Good, and do let me know if there is. This is how we become better educated about economics through the work of historians of economic thought.

> Others admit that if a nation could be separated from all the world, it would be of no consequence how much, or how little money circulated in it. The consumable goods which were circulated by means of this money would only be exchanged for a greater or a smaller number of pieces; but the real wealth or poverty of the country, they allow, would depend altogether upon the abundance or scarcity of those consumable goods. But it is otherwise, they think, with countries which have connections with foreign nations, and which are obliged to carry on foreign wars, and to maintain fleets and armies in distant countries. This, they say, cannot be done but by sending abroad money to pay them with; and a nation cannot send much money abroad unless it has a good deal at home. Every such nation, therefore, must endeavour in time of peace to accumulate gold and silver that, when occasion requires, it may have wherewithal to carry on foreign wars. (Ibid.: 451–2)

Adam Smith's primary aim in drawing this historical contrast is to ridicule an ancient belief and replace it with what he will argue is a far better conception. It is trade that matters, and gold and silver, if used wisely, will repay their expenditure with an even larger inflow in the fullness of time.

There is a second example from Smith. Here again, but in this case in defending his own set of arguments, Smith goes into the past to look at the views of a different economist, in this case at the writings of Thomas Mun in his 1664 *England's Treasure by Forraign Trade*. He quotes Mun in comparing the liberal use of gold and silver in foreign trade to the use by farmers of seed corn in planting crops:

> If we only behold, [says he] the actions of the husbandman in the seed-time, when he casteth away much good corn into the ground, we shall account him rather a madman than a husbandman. But when we consider his labours in the harvest, which is the end of his endeavours, we shall find the worth and plentiful increase of his action. (Ibid.: 453)

A third example. In the next great revolution in economics, it is Adam Smith himself who is held up as the example of an economist of the past whose impaired understanding has stood in the way of the development of sound economic theory. The marginal revolution rode in many ways on the back of the diamond–water paradox which had been initially discussed in the *Wealth of Nations*. There Smith wrote:

> The word VALUE, it is to be observed, has two different meanings, and sometimes expresses the utility of some particular object, and sometimes the power of purchasing other goods which the possession of that object conveys. The one may be called "value in use"; the other, "value in exchange." The things which have the greatest value in use have frequently little or no value in exchange; those which have the greatest value in exchange have frequently little or no use value. Nothing is more useful than water: but it will purchase scarce any thing; scarce any thing can be had in exchange for it. A diamond, on the contrary, has scarce any value in use; but a very great quantity of other goods may frequently be had in exchange for it. (Ibid.: 33)

In the standard account, it was William Stanley Jevons, in his *Theory of Political Economy*, who seized on this passage in Smith to discuss the actual nature of value within economic theory. In contrasting marginal analysis with the approach adopted by Smith and the classical school, Jevons countered Smith:

> From this confusion has arisen much perplexity. Many of those commodities which are the most useful to us are esteemed and desired the least. We cannot live a day without water, and yet in ordinary circumstances we set no value on it. Why is this? Simply because we usually have so much of it that its final degree of utility is reduced nearly to zero. (Jevons [1871] 1888: 62)

And the unravelling of this paradox was in an understanding of final (that is, marginal) utility:

> We shall seldom need to consider the degree of utility except as regards the last increment which has been consumed, or, which comes to the same thing, the next increment which is about to be consumed. I shall therefore commonly use the expression final degree of utility, as meaning the degree of utility of the last addition, or the next possible addition of a very small, or infinitely small, quantity to the existing stock. (Ibid.: 51)

Dwelling on Smith's by then almost one-hundred-year-old reasoning was an important part of the process in Jevons arriving at a different, more coherent theory of value.

Possibly the most dramatic use made of economists of the past in effecting a profound change in economic theory occurred as an intrinsic part of the Keynesian revolution. It is even worth wondering whether without the historical discussion that preceded the theoretical arguments, the theories that Keynes was proposing would have gained such wide and immediate acceptance.

Central to Keynes's arguments was a historical analysis of Ricardian economics versus Malthusian. Keynes returned to the early nineteenth century to find the proper mode of thinking in addressing the problems of the Great Depression as he understood them. Keynes was, moreover, quite clear about the need to look at the problems of recession in a way similar to the approach adopted by Malthus and to reject the way in which they were analysed by Ricardo. In writing to Harlan McCracken in 1933, Keynes, who was at the time in the early stages of the *General Theory*, wrote that "in the matter of Malthus … I wholly agree with you in regarding him as a much under-estimated pioneer in the line of thought which to-day seems to me by far the most likely to lead to progress in the analysis of the business cycle" (Kates 2010: 44). This same idea was expressed in the *General Theory* in a famous early passage in which the consequences of adopting Ricardo's line of thought is contrasted with the might-have-been had Malthus's been the seed from which economic theory sprang.

> The idea that we can safely neglect the aggregate demand function is fundamental to the Ricardian economics, which underlie what we have been taught for more than a century. Malthus, indeed, had vehemently opposed Ricardo's doctrine that it was impossible for effective demand to be deficient; but vainly. For, since Malthus was unable to explain clearly (apart from an appeal to the facts of common observation) how and why effective demand could be deficient or excessive, he failed to furnish an alternative construction; and Ricardo conquered England as completely as the Holy Inquisition conquered Spain. Not only was his theory accepted by the city, by statesmen and by the academic world. But controversy ceased; the other point of view completely disappeared; it ceased to be discussed. The great puzzle of Effective Demand with which Malthus had wrestled vanished from economic literature. You will not find it mentioned even once in the whole works of Marshall, Edgeworth and Professor Pigou, from whose hands the classical theory has received its most mature embodiment. It could only live on furtively, below the surface, in the underworlds of Karl Marx, Silvio Gesell or Major Douglas. (Keynes [1936] 1973: 32)

This is Keynes turning to historical examples as a means of showing how his own theory differed from the theories of those who had come before. He argued that, even at the time he was writing in 1936, the contrast between Ricardo and Malthus remained of immediate concern. It was Malthus who had tried to show that demand deficiency was a probable cause of recession and involuntary unemployment. It was Ricardo who had disagreed. Keynes's intention in drawing this analogy was to clarify the relevant issues for his own contemporaries.

Yet as much as the use of history in setting economics in a new direction was based on a discussion of the economics of the past, this is, in fact, far and away the weakest argument in support of the study of HET. Since revolutionary changes in the direction of economic thought are extremely rare, with about a century between Smith and Jevons and more than sixty years between Jevons and Keynes, there is no serious case to be made for the study of HET as the potential spark that would lead to the overturning of economic theory and the introduction of a new direction in the understanding of economic relationships.

This is not to deny that Smith's concern with "mercantilist" thinking was an important catalyst for writing the *Wealth of Nations*, or that the diamond–water paradox was not something that Jevons was pleased to see more clearly explained using marginal analysis, or that Keynes's discovery of Malthus and rejection of Ricardo may have been crucial to his outlining the need to introduce aggregate demand. They may well have been just as important as is sometimes argued, or they may have been completely unimportant. But whichever is the case, it is not anything like a justification for having all economists study the economists of the past.

Indeed, the historical arguments may well have been the least important element in causing economic theory to move in a new direction in all three of these major instances from the history of economic theory. Each of these stories forms part of the mythology of each of these major departures in economic analysis, but their value may be greater in teaching economics than as a basis for believing that HET could be instrumental in revolutionary shifts in the theory and practice of economics.

ORIENTATION FOR THE DEVELOPMENT OF THEORY

A completely different argument, however, looks at the role of an understanding of HET in giving direction to evolutionary developments in economic theory. Revolutionary episodes though there may supposedly be, economics more usually develops incrementally in response to the conditions of the world. There is a continuous testing of existing theory against the realities as found within the economy, with a feedback process a spontaneous aspect of the way in which theory and actual circumstance interact.

Theory is never perfectly structured to begin with, but even if it were, conditions change. There is therefore continuous advantage in reflecting on the theoretical structures that have survived into the present, with a view to shaping these so that their application will more accurately fit the contours of a specific period. Such reflection on existing theory is undertaken by a significant proportion of academic economists in all areas of the discipline. That is a large part of what university-based economists are expected to do. They think about how to think about economic issues.

Dissatisfaction with whatever happens to be the mainstream theory of the time has been a perennial issue for as long as economies have been studied. Theory is never just a settled body of conclusions. It is always and everywhere a set of conclusions together with the process by which those conclusions were reached. The history of the development of the theory is itself an important ingredient in understanding what those theories mean in practice, as well as being part of the typical methodology in advancing beyond whatever conclusions represent the reigning conceptual framework of the moment.

Economists regularly use past theories to frame issues for the future. There is, in fact, nothing else to use. Economics will at every moment have an existing body of knowledge and theory that has evolved out of the past. There will be a standard textbook theoretical explanation covering most economic questions and a generally accepted ruling framework for applying such theory in particular circumstances. But there will also be at every moment some dissatisfaction with the standard answers because the certainty is that they cannot cover every contingency nor every aspect of every problem.

An instructive example of the role of the history of economics in the development of economic theory was provided in the Presidential Address to the American Economics Association that was delivered in January 2007. The outgoing AEA President, George Akerlof, a Nobel Prize-winning economist, spoke on "The Missing Motivation in Macroeconomics".

What follows below is the Introduction to Akerlof's address. His intention was to push macroeconomics in a new direction, but the approach adopted in trying to convince his fellow economists of the need for change was to review the relevant developments in macroeconomic theory that had taken place over the previous forty years. The entire address did no more than amplify the following introductory statement which is included at length since it demonstrates, paragraph after paragraph, how singularly important the historical narrative can be. The extended quotation should not be seen as an endorsement of the content, only of the use of the history of economics to provide orientation in the present as well as momentum towards a change in theoretical direction.

> Macroeconomics changed between the early 1960s and the late 1970s. The macroeconomics of the early 1960s was avowedly Keynesian. This was manifested in the textbooks of the time, which showed a remarkable unity from the introductory through the graduate levels. John Maynard Keynes appeared, posthumously, on the cover of Time Magazine. Even Milton Friedman was famously – although perhaps misleadingly – quoted, "We are all Keynesians now." A little more than a decade later Robert Lucas and Thomas Sargent (1979) had published "After Keynesian Macroeconomics." The love-fest was over.
>
> The decline of the old-style Keynesian economics was due in part to the simultaneous rise in inflation and unemployment in the late 1960s and early 1970s. That occurrence was impossible to reconcile with the simple non-accelerationist Phillips Curves of the time.
>
> But Keynesian economics also declined because of a change in economic methodology. The Keynesians had emphasized the dependence of consumption on disposable income, and similarly, of investment on current profits and current cash flow. They posited a Phillips Curve, where nominal – rather than real – wage inflation depended upon the unemployment rate, which was used as an indication of the looseness of the labor market. They based these functions on their own introspection

> regarding how the various actors in the economy would behave. They also brought some discipline into their judgments by estimating statistical relations.
>
> But a new school of thought, based on classical economics, objected to the casual ways of these folks. New Classical critics of Keynesian economics insisted instead that these relations be derived from fundamentals. They said that macroeconomic relationships should be derived from profit-maximizing by firms and from utility-maximizing by consumers with economic arguments in their utility functions.
>
> The new methodology had a profound effect on macroeconomics. Five separate neutrality results overturned aspects of macroeconomics that Keynesians had previously considered incontestable. These five neutralities are: the independence of consumption and current income (the life-cycle permanent income hypothesis); the irrelevance of current profits to investment spending (the Modigliani-Miller theorem); the long-run independence of inflation and unemployment (natural rate theory); the inability of monetary policy to stabilize output (the Rational Expectations hypothesis); and the irrelevance of taxes and budget deficits to consumption (Ricardian equivalence). These results fly in the face of Keynesian economics. They undermine its conclusions about the behavior of the economy and the impact of stabilization policy.
>
> The discovery of these five neutrality propositions surprised macroeconomists. They had not suspected that radically anti-Keynesian conclusions were the logical outcome of such seemingly innocuous maximizing assumptions. (Akerlof 2007: 3–4)

This is economics as it is practised at the very highest levels. This is the development of a new theoretical direction whose arguments are founded on a review of the previous theories. No one listening to this speech would dismiss it as nothing more than an excursion into the history of economics and therefore irrelevant to economics. Indeed, it was widely reproduced and discussed because of what it said about the direction that economics must take. Whether it succeeded in changing the direction of the practice of economics is, of course, a different matter. But what ought to be crystal clear is that the methodology used was to review the relevant history of thought and then draw conclusions on the direction that economic theory should follow.

Without the background history such an approach is an impossibility. A listener without knowledge of the history cannot gauge the accuracy of what is being said. A familiarity with the history of economics should therefore be recognised as an intrinsic part of the necessary knowledge base for anyone thinking about theoretical issues. Akerlof assumed that those who listened to his address would understand the history well enough to understand the direction in which he wished to see economic theory progress. It was therefore important for all concerned that they did have the historical knowledge required to make sense of the arguments being presented.

A CONVERSATION WITH ECONOMISTS OF THE PAST

The shallow and sterile formalism of so much of modern economics, an outcome driven in part by the nature of the publication formats of the modern journal, has tended to flatten debate and remove much of the passion that was a feature of earlier days. For all the undoubted changes that have occurred economies are not so very different today from how they were in the past. Economists from what some may consider bygone eras have something to say to us, and listening to them can contribute to our understanding.

By focusing only on the writers of the present or near-present, we deny ourselves the opportunity to listen to the views of economists from earlier times who had much to say about the economies of their own time that has application in the economies of our own. An interesting reminder that this was once well understood amongst the economics profession may be seen in Professor Hartley Withers's introduction to a 1915 reprint of Walter Bagehot's *Lombard Street: A Description of the Money Market*, which was first published in 1873. Some forty-two years after *Lombard Street*'s publication, this is how Professor Withers, himself a monetary economist of high repute in his own time, describes the value of Bagehot's book in a frontispiece to the volume:

> The English credit system is a living thing, that has grown out of its past and is growing into its future. Past, present, and future are thus one continuing process, and no one can hope to understand its present, still less to peer into its future, unless he knows something of the past that is part of them. Bagehot's "Lombard Street" lights up, with the fire of its author's genius, the road that we have travelled, and helps us see where we are and to wonder whither we are going. (Withers in Bagehot [1873] 1915: iii)

The nesting of Bagehot within Withers, who both have something to say to us all these years later about the management of the financial system, is a reminder that valuable insights are there to be had by those who bother to look. But as a further nesting you, the reader, are reading this in yet another time period, with a wholly different surrounding set of circumstances. Yet Withers's recommendation to read Bagehot has a relevance that is almost certainly perennial. It is hard to imagine a future in which reading Bagehot would not be useful to economists. An approach to economics that sees no value in becoming acquainted with the perspectives of the past, from economists of genius who were dealing with phenomena intrinsically little different from the ones we deal with now, severs the profession from a fuller understanding of different ways of reading the operation of an economy.

That, too, is the role of HET. It is to bring into the conversation the views of economists of the past. As modern and up-to-date as we think of ourselves, one day we will be as long gone as Bagehot or Withers. It would be extraordinarily sad indeed to believe that nothing any of us write, say or do will have any enduring value other than through its being absorbed via a process of osmosis into the general economic ideas of some future time. We should want to be part of the economic conversations of the future in the same way that we should welcome our own economic ancestors into our own conversations today. Not because we are being polite to the elderly, but because they have something useful to tell us that speaks to our own present concerns.

A STOREHOUSE OF ECONOMIC IDEAS

Textbook theory provides a compendium of the theoretical approaches that have gained currency at some particular point in time. But for every theory accepted there are others that were close competitors in their time, some of which would now be seen as utterly beyond the pale while others remain highly suggestive. The social sciences are very different from the natural sciences in this respect. A theory might find its way into the textbooks because the issues it addressed had currency at the time, but as different economic problems become more prominent, theories that might formerly have been overlooked can have something important to contribute.

Indeed, the very way in which the losing sides in so many of these controversies continue to contest the field provides an important part of the ongoing debate within economics. The following statement from John Stuart Mill is an interesting and instructive example of the value of returning to re-examine even the most settled of economic questions. In touching on one such issue, Mill wrote:

> These general principles are now well understood by almost all who profess to have studied the subject, and are disputed by few except those who ostentatiously proclaim their contempt for such studies. We touch upon the question, not in the hope of rendering these fundamental truths clearer than they already are, but to perform a task, so useful and needful, that it is to be wished it were oftener deemed part of the business of those who direct their assaults against ancient prejudices, – *that of seeing that no scattered particles of important truth are buried and lost in the ruins of exploded error*. (Mill [1874] 1974: para II 6 – italics added)

As it happens, the "general principles [which according to Mill] are now well understood" are what is today known as Say's Law. At the time Mill wrote, the virtually unanimous view within the economics profession was that Say's Law was valid. Mill was pointing out that despite this near universal acceptance it was worth looking at the opposing arguments just to see what might turn up. A century later, and indeed up to this very day (2013), that particular principle is almost universally rejected. There is agreement across the profession that Say's Law is false. Whether this will always be the case, who can know? But whether any particular theory is taken to be valid or not, it is only through Mill's "useful and needful" task of re-examination that discarded theories can be reassessed, reinterpreted and where it is thought appropriate, reintroduced into the mainstream, to ensure that, as Mill wrote, "no scattered particles of important truth are buried and lost".

Indeed, this is precisely what Keynes did in combing through Malthus's writings and coming to a conclusion that has been generally accepted throughout the economics mainstream, that there had indeed been a valid form of economic understanding that lay unappreciated in the works of this early nineteenth-century economist. From these roots a revolution in economic theory arose. The economists of the past are custodians of a repository of theories and observations with relevance and application today.

There are also ideas that have been put forward that may have been before their time. The circumstances for their acceptance hadn't existed when they were first presented or the related ideas that were necessary for their acceptance had not been brought into the conversation. A familiarity with historic ideas and a mindset that does not automatically disregard such thoughts because they are old are necessary ingredients in bringing such ideas to light. This, too, is what an understanding of the history of economic thought allows to happen.

A LITERARY APPROACH TO ECONOMIC ISSUES

The ebbing role of the history of economic thought within economics generally is in many respects a reflection of the ascendancy of mathematical and statistical approaches. As those with a historical perspective on economics well understand, there has been a long, on-going debate over the proper role of numbers, equations and time series within the overall structure of economic theorising and practice. Much of the debate had originally taken place within a tradition that had placed great value on a literate economics community. Marshall in 1890 discussed the role of mathematics in the preface to the first edition of his *Principles* in which he famously left the mathematics to the appendix. Of this decision, he wrote:

> The chief use of pure mathematics in economic questions seems to be in helping a person to write down quickly, shortly and exactly, some of his thoughts for his own use: and to make sure that he has enough, and only enough, premisses for his conclusions (i.e. that his equations are neither more nor less in number than his unknowns). But when a great many symbols have to be used, they become very laborious to any one but the writer himself. … It seems doubtful whether any one spends his time well in reading lengthy translations of economic doctrines into mathematics, that have not been made by themselves. (Marshall [1920] 1947: x–xi)

Similarly, Keynes in the *General Theory* wrote that,

> Too large a proportion of recent "mathematical" economics are merely concoctions, as imprecise as the initial assumptions they rest on, which allow the author to lose sight of the complexities and interdependencies of the real world in a maze of pretentious and unhelpful symbols. (Keynes [1936] 1973: 297)

For some, quoting such authorities on the dangerous role of highly mathematical techniques and requirements in economic theory may do no more than make a virtue of necessity where the requisite skills are in limited supply. But the reality is that economists must communicate with others in situations where the common language is the normal discourse of words.

Perhaps even more importantly, much of what drives an economy cannot be reduced to only those sorts of considerations that can be expressed numerically. Issues must often be conceptualised in ways that bring in subtle shades of meaning. This is an ability that can only be developed through practice and craft.

A study of the history of economic thought brings into the remit of contemporary economists some of the finest writers in the history of our subject. Their rhetorical abilities, in many ways, underlie the continuing influence of their work on later generations. Those who can establish their points most clearly are best able to carry others along with them. The ability to write well has undoubtedly had an important influence on the direction that economics has taken. Many of the great economists were also recognised as great writers: Adam Smith, John Stuart Mill, Karl Marx, Alfred Marshall, John Maynard Keynes, Friedrich Hayek. Each was a writer of genius whose ability to write persuasively played a large part in their ability to influence others.

Studying the great economists of the past and publishing on the history of economic thought develops one's writing skills. But more than this, it develops one's skills in writing logically about economics. Specialists in the history of economic thought typically handle theoretical questions but in doing so they learn to explain concepts in words, an extremely important skill too often downplayed within economics generally.

A TRAINING GROUND FOR APPLIED ECONOMISTS

Much of the discussion of the role of HET revolves around its uses within the academic world – based, it seems, on the tacit assumption that teaching and research are the sole and final ends of economics. In reality, economics is a policy science whose ultimate role is to provide a sufficiently deep theoretical understanding of the structure of economies to allow for the making of sound economic decisions. To underestimate the powerful role of studying the history of economic thought in the training of economists whose work is in government or the private sector is to misunderstand the way in which economists can and do become economists.

Students of HET have in most cases focused on some particular branch of economic theory. Upon graduation many are employed as economists, and within their role will retain a deeper understanding of economic theory as well as the limits of such theory.

All economists today learn modern macroeconomic and microeconomic theory. Virtually every serious student of economics also studies mathematical and statistical techniques, often to a very high standard. A study of the history of economics isn't a substitute for the study of economics; it is a sub-branch within the overall discipline and in this sense should be understood as one of the pathways towards becoming an economist and learning the tools of the trade.

It is entirely possible that HET has often been taught inappropriately, given its value as a contribution to economics as a practical art. But we have gone from teaching the history of their discipline to virtually all economists to teaching it to virtually none and in that change a very important component in the education of an economist has disappeared. It is, of course, the case that no practising economist is ever asked to settle a question in the history of theory; instead they are asked to come up with practical answers to often very difficult real-world problems. The contention here is that those who have studied the history of theory are able to access a wider range of answers and are better able to think outside the necessarily more narrow confines of whatever the reigning paradigm of the present moment happens to be.

A PATHWAY TO UNDERSTANDING ECONOMIC THEORY AND ITS APPLICATION

The history of economic thought has a long history as a teaching tool.

Because it is so useful as an expository device, students are taught at least in some vague fashion the marginal revolution, wherein a comparison between the concept of total utility employed by earlier theorists gave way to an analysis that concerned itself with the addition to value of the last item bought. Marshall in his *Principles* repeatedly referred to economists of an earlier time in discussing various topics.[2] What these represent are examples of a knowledge of HET as a means of explaining modern theory by comparing it with the theories of the past.

The reason for such an approach is fairly straightforward. Putting two (or more) theories side by side for comparison provides a background frame of reference. One of the theories is considered better, more complete, more encompassing while the other is seen as inferior, less complete, not as useful. In understanding the difference between the two, the features of the more favoured theory are clarified and brought into focus.

This is in many ways the traditional use for a historical understanding. It enables the economist to employ the "mistaken" theories of the past as a background against which to understand modern theory. Mark Blaug in his path-breaking *Economic Theory in Retrospect* makes that point in the very first paragraph of his preface:

> This book is a study of the logical coherence and explanatory value of what has come to be known as orthodox economic theory. The history of this body of received doctrine goes back at least as far as Adam Smith. I am not concerned, however, with historical antecedents for their own sake. My purpose is to teach contemporary economic theory. (Blaug 1968: ix)

---

[2] See, for example, his chapter 3 of Book I on "Gradations of Consumers' Demand" where he refers to the work of Ricardo, Gossen, John Stuart Mill, Cairnes, Cournot and Dupuit (Marshall [1920] 1947: 92–101).

There is nothing in any of this to suggest that even the most modern up-to-date theory will not itself one day be held up as an example of some woebegone half-truth, mistruth or outright error. It is merely a device for allowing those being taught in the here and now to appreciate in finer detail what is modern by seeing it against what has been transcended. In seeing the differences, a learning process takes place. By holding up for examination what are considered mistaken rudimentary theoretical approaches for dealing with particular economic issues, the various aspects of what should be avoided are brought to light.

Although this may seem a form of intellectual arrogance, it is not. None of us believe that any of what we write and say provides the last word. We are just the most recent manifestation of a long process of theoretical development. We merely use the theories of the past as a framework in which to highlight the features of the new.

The singular utility of HET as a means to understand economic theory is tacitly acknowledged in the literature reviews almost invariably included as part of the doctoral thesis. In answering the question whether the candidate has absorbed everything of consequence written in the field, there is a tacit appreciation of the value of the knowledge gained in undertaking this part of the research. We therefore implicitly make it clear that this is how economists learn to be economists. We learn from watching how others had grappled with similar problems in the past. We recognise that before one can make a fresh contribution of one's own, it is imperative to have understood what contributions others have already made.

AN ALTERNATIVE PATHWAY FOR TEACHING ECONOMIC THEORY AND ITS APPLICATION

When does the work of an economist pass from the contemporary world into the historic? At what point does someone's work no longer count as modern but is instead seen as having entered the pantheon of the great but unread? It is also an interesting but opposite question to ask who determines what is modern economics and what is not. Is "modern" determined by the editors of journals or by textbook writers? Is modernity in the questions being asked or is it in the answers being given? Who decides whether an economic theory or form of presentation has passed its use-by date or whether it remains part of the immediate present? When is an economic answer to an economic question no longer the right answer and where can one find out? Are there some questions that are themselves now part of the history of economic theory while others still remain alive? Is it just the way the texts are written that determines whether they are in fashion or out? Or is it, as one would hope in an incremental science, the answers themselves that make the difference? Is it whether the presentation is highly mathematical, or graphical or philosophical that separates the modern from the old? Is it grammar and style of writing?

Continuing in this same vein, what must an economist know to be an economist? What is the minimal expectation of employers or their fellow economists? What would their expectations be of the base knowledge of another economist with whom they must discuss and work? What would a student's own expectations be?

What would the minimum educational requirement of an economist consist of? Would a working knowledge of these suffice?

- scarcity and the need for trade-offs
- opportunity cost
- marginal utility and the theory of value
- the role of markets
- supply and demand
- marginal revenue, marginal cost and the theory of the firm
- welfare economics and externalities
- causes of and cures for unemployment
- causes of and cures for inflation
- interest rates and the role of money.

There is more, of course, but anyone with a sound working knowledge of the modern textbook answers to these issues would and could function as an economist. This could not be taught to a professional standard in a single year, even if a principles course might acquaint a student with each and every one of these topics. And in a typical course they would be taught horizontally as an embodiment of the present state of economic theory.

But if someone were interested in economics but had no desire to pursue an economics career, there is no necessary reason to teach these matters horizontally, that is, with no historical development but as the final conclusions. They could just as easily be taught vertically where the framework for the course material would be the historical development of each of these areas. These are ideas that have a historic presence as part of the history of economics, some elements existing right from the start, such as scarcity (which is found in the index of *The Wealth of Nations*) and others which have a more recent provenance (such as marginal analysis). Dealing with these topics inside of a single semester would not be a gigantic task while at the end of such a course students would have a unique and lively understanding of economic theory. They would not be economists, but if taught with an appreciation of why such answers to economic questions had arisen in the first place along with what today's answers to those questions might be, they would be better equipped to deal with economic matters than many students would have who do no more than a single principles course.

But at the same time, even those who would like to work as economists would benefit from such a course in the history of these ideas. There is value in the personal orientation within economic theory, for an economist to understand these concepts through a knowledge of how they were conceived and the circumstances in which they were developed, within a rigorous and necessary framework of debate and discussion. Such a course would give life to those concepts that merely teaching economics horizontally cannot do. This would not necessarily have to be the introductory principles course, although it could be. It would instead be part of an undergraduate degree in which economic theory was teased out of its historical evolution. And for students who have already undertaken economic studies, such a course would hardly be redundant to the knowledge they already have but would provide a complement to that knowledge, allowing the development and maturation of the conceptual framework that they hold.[3]

[3] Chapter 5 provides a discussion of the suggested methodology for teaching the history of economic thought.

THE HISTORY OF ECONOMIC THOUGHT MAKES AN ECONOMIST A BETTER ECONOMIST

The question of questions remains. If an economist-in-training studies the history of economic thought, do the benefits outweigh the opportunity cost? Because of the time spent on HET, do they end up not having the time to learn what would in the longer run have been more valuable? Will they miss the maths and stats they could have learned instead? Will having a more historical orientation and an understanding of the literary traditions in economics compensate them for the knowledge they might have gathered in some other course?

This is a question that no one can answer with any certainty on either side. But this much can be said: there is a distinct and sizeable loss in the capabilities of any economist who does not study the history of economics. Their theoretical abilities are less polished. They have less understanding of the theories they apply. They are not as competent at handling philosophical and conceptual issues. They will not have the same skills as they might have had in being able to read economic material for meaning and at expressing their views coherently in writing. They are less aware of the vast amount of material that already exists that might be useful to them in dealing with the questions they will be asked to answer. They are not as likely to be able to think historically either in relation to the ideas they use or in the way in which historical events unfolded. They are less likely to seek out material in the works of older economists whose writing they have not been taught to respect. They will not even be as likely to know which economists they might have turned to for stimulation and assistance. They will be trapped in the present with no means to seek out alternative perspectives even if it occurred to them to look.

They are, to put it simply, less capable as economists. They may be able to function and even thrive in certain environments, but by no means in all. They will have been deprived of the depth and breadth that historical studies provide and will not even be aware of their deprivation. They will understand less and be less capable of succeeding in certain areas of work that economists are frequently asked to undertake.

Studying the history of economic theory makes someone a better economist. That is why it should be taught to everyone who studies economics or at a minimum offered to them as an option. If it didn't make someone a better economist, there would be little reason to ask economists to undertake this kind of study. But it does make them better economists, and it also makes them better scholars. An economist without the kinds of knowledge that HET provides, so far as their role as economists is concerned, is no better than a tradesman. They may be able to run a regression but they are not scholars as it was once understood.[4]

Economics is part of the social sciences with a long history of philosophical development that preceded its more technical aspects, even though they now live side-by-side. A complete economist must understand the technical, philosophical and historical aspects of economics – which is a study of actual economies as they exist in the world, inhabited as they are by individual human beings who must collaborate with each other in a social framework to produce the goods and services they collectively consume. Learning the history of economics is one of the most important ways in which the non-technical philosophical side of economics can be studied and learned.

And to go beyond the benefits to the economist as an individual, the benefit to the entire cohort of economists is profound. Each of us benefits from the knowledge and skills of others. The division of labour even applies to knowledge. Economists with a knowledge of the history of economic thought are a resource. All economists benefit because some economists know the historic roots and

---

[4] In this regard, I might mention a conversation I had with a PhD student about his doctorate. It dealt with development policy in Country X and he was working on a data set that had been compiled by an international agency. So I asked if he had contacted the government of Country X to let them know he was working on this project since it might be of interest to them and they might be able to help him out. No, he hadn't and couldn't really see why he would bother. Well, had he gone to Country X? No, he hadn't. Well was he intending to go to Country X to see what things are like on the ground? No he wasn't and the idea that he might seemed utterly fantastic to him. So that's what economics now is, at least for some. Not working on problems about people, but developing a skill set that would allow them to manipulate a dataset. The issues in their social, historical and philosophical setting are not necessarily the core driving interest. How typical this is I cannot tell.

origins of the theories we apply. It increases the power of economists in general to solve the economic problems we are asked to deal with.

3. Debating the role of the history of economic thought

> Economics does not merely have a lot to learn from history: history is what it is.
>
> (D.N. McCloskey 1986: 69)

Aside from the general indifference to the subject that now prevails within departments of economics, there are, broadly speaking, three overlapping groups against which the history of economic thought as it now exists must be actively defended. Two of these groups are attempting to do what in their view is best for the subject. I don't agree with their approach but it is not intended to do harm, although I believe it would. The third of these would gladly see HET outside of economics completely and would be content to see historians of economics no longer classified as economists. I will discuss this third group first.

HOSTILITY FROM THE MAINSTREAM

The safest kind of history of economics is what has been described as Whig history. Everything that came before the present must be, by assumption, inferior. No attempt should therefore be made to use the history of economics as part of an argument for reform, not because we cannot learn from the past but because it will create hostility amongst the mainstream. Roy Weintraub discusses the position of those who advise the use of HET as part of an argument intended as a criticism of some particular aspect of mainstream theory.

> Suppose historians of economics were to take this advice. I submit that the history of economics would soon stand in the same relation to economics as creationism does to evolutionary biology. "They will be held in contempt" is too weak a forecast of the position of a small band

> of outsiders that sets itself up to criticize the fundamental analyses of a dominant scientific elite. If most economists understand the history of economics as an attack on mainstream economics, they will be hostile to the subdiscipline and its claims on common resources of faculty positions and student time. (Weintraub 2002: 6)

This is a sound observation and I suspect that a goodly part of the retreat that has been suffered by the history of economic thought has occurred for just that reason. There is a wariness about HET within the mainstream that extends into an open hostility. But whatever else the history of economics might be, it can never just be Whig history. There will always be some who study the economics of the past who come to believe that there is relevance for the modern world in what had been written at some earlier time. The history of economics therefore contains by its nature a different perspective on economic theory, methodology and the appropriate policies to adopt in different circumstances. Suppressing this aspect of HET may reduce the hostility of the mainstream by some small amount but it is hard to see how acting in this way has improved the standing of the history of economic thought.

Thus with those who see an enemy of some sort within the history of economics, the indifference of the economics profession to its own history in general has expanded beyond neutrality to the extent that the history of economics is identified as a refuge for economists who do not accept the mainstream neo-classical paradigm found in the modern textbook. It is seen by some as a gathering place of malcontents who use the history of economics as a platform from which to criticise mainstream economic theory and policy. For such economists, the history of economics is no longer the dispassionate study of ancient ways of thinking but a breeding ground for those who would seek to tear down the carefully constructed edifice of modern economics.

Such concerns are by no means invalid. To varying degrees conferences on the history of economics do attract papers from all strands of the economic spectrum whose membership does maintain an active interest in the history of their subject even if, often enough, that interest is largely confined to the particular school to which they belong. There is therefore a concern among mainstream economists that maintaining the history of economics within the overall economics classification not only brings into the subject opposing sets of paradigms but gives these groups a respectability they do not deserve. There is, as a result, an active resistance to the continuance of the history of economics within the discipline by some of the leaders of the profession.

Contributing to this attempt to distance economics from its history is the degree to which HET tends towards the philosophical and literary side of the economics tradition, which makes it out of phase with the modern fashion. The history of economics does not have a mathematical or econometric element of any consequence. The theorists who tend to be discussed not only are mainly from the literary tradition, but even where there are histories of mathematical economics, game theory, econometrics or other such technical approaches, the tendency is still to discuss this history using the more literary or philosophical approach of an older form of economic discourse. Although some have used mathematics to discuss HET – Mark Blaug and Paul Samuelson come to mind – it is not the norm. To many economists today, these examples of non-mathematical discussion should not be classified as economics.

The end result is that the history of economic thought is seen by some not as benign and useful but rather as a force for harm. If they could rid economic theory of its historians, they would do so. In their own minds, there is no offsetting positive. They do not agree with John Stuart Mill on the value of re-examining older theories as a means of "seeing that no scattered particles of important truth are buried and lost in the ruins of exploded error". Weintraub is possibly right in his assessment of the attitude by some proportion of the profession to historical debates that impinge on modern theory. But rather than that being a reason for trying to diminish that aspect of HET, perhaps it is a reason to encourage it. Given how rapidly the teaching of the history of economic thought has been disappearing, it is hard to see that HET could travel any worse than it already is if it were seen to embody an element of danger for a complacent mainstream.

PLACATING THE MAINSTREAM

Given that there are those within the mainstream who would like to see the history of economic thought disappear because of its role as a locus for criticism of economic theory as it now is, there have been two strategies developed to protect and preserve HET. The first of these strategies has sought accommodation by ensuring to the largest extent possible that HET is not used to criticise mainstream economics. The aim is to keep scholarship in the history of economic thought as docile and unthreatening as possible. Not that such an outcome is possible, but that is the aim. HET by its very nature fosters dissatisfaction with aspects of mainstream economic ideas. Studying the views of earlier economists can lead at least some economists to prefer these earlier ideas in place of those taught in mainstream texts. In addition, the history of economic thought attracts a large proportion from amongst the heterodox who frame economic theory in a different way from the mainstream and who tend to reach conclusions that would not be supported by mainstream analysis. And not only do such economists have interesting and valuable contributions to make about the way in which economic theory developed, each of the various heterodox traditions has a history of its own as a sub-branch of the history of economic thought in general which it values and seeks to discuss. The history of economic thought is therefore seen as providing a cover of respectability for scholars who otherwise could not find their work included within any other branch of orthodox economic analysis.

Given also that those who study the history of economic thought are often critics of the mainstream, this is either a problem in itself because it unnecessarily weakens the authority of economics in general, or a meta-problem which exists only because there are many highly placed economists who resent this criticism but whose concerns must be taken into account by historians of economics. And it may even be the case that many if not most historians of economics are also part of the mainstream and do not themselves appreciate the use of HET as a means of criticising existing economic theory. But whichever it is, one of the ways to deal with this is to limit the use of HET as a battleground for theory and economic policy. An economist from one of the heterodox traditions can examine the development of ideas within a historical context but, it is argued, must not use the history of economics as a means to debate economic theory. That is what journals outside the history of economics are designed to do. Within HET, it is better to leave this particular hornet's nest undisturbed. To ensure that the study of the history of economics occurs on neutral ground, historians of economics should avoid any issues that buy into contemporary debates or attempt to use their history in that way. They are welcome to use history as part of a discussion within the mainstream but when practising as a historian of economics, such divisive issues should be avoided.

This is more than just an attempt to keep the peace. Historians of economics are a diverse group of economists whose interests are often, in miniature, aspects of the vast body of economic theory. No issue in relation to the future direction of economics can be determined by looking at its past. Debates over theory should be fought out amongst theoreticians who are specialists in the particular area. It is therefore argued that allowing theoretical or policy debates to intrude on the history of economics achieves nothing other than raising further the disdain of the mainstream, making the history of economics less secure within economics because it loses the support of many who would be indulgent of a more disinterested study.

For anyone interested in the future development of HET these are extremely important considerations. Although it is seldom explicitly stated in just that way, those who use historical knowledge to contest mainstream theory are seen as gatecrashers and uninvited guests. Although I see part of the role of the history of economics as a means of examining and testing mainstream theory, it is not hard to see why allowing the history of economics to invade policy debate is so unwelcome. This is a legitimate concern and it is impossible to say who is right. If HET were more secure than it is, then this would be an acceptable part of what historians of economics would be seen to do. But with it already in such a weak position, it may be right to keep it as inconspicuous as possible as a tactic for survival. It may even be right in principle and would be the case even if HET were widely taught and respected. Defining the role it should play and understanding its confines is a genuine issue. I will merely note that those who seek to constrain the history of economic thought within this confined space may be doing the subject more harm than good since it makes the area less interesting to others and also less valuable. But that is my judgement and it is a judgement not universally shared.

THE HISTORY OF ECONOMIC THOUGHT AS THE HISTORY AND PHILOSOPHY OF SCIENCE

The second strategy designed to protect and preserve HET is closely related to the approach just discussed. This group is made up of historians of economics who recognise that their days as a sub-discipline within economics may be numbered and are looking for a new home. They believe that economists have so completely dispensed with the history of economic thought that rather than wait to be discarded, historians of economics should decamp en masse and join with historians of science. The history of economic thought would then no longer be seen as part of economics, which for many economists it no longer is.

It is, moreover, not merely a fringe grouping of historians of economic thought who wish to make this trek; the idea has been discussed and promoted by some of the most influential members of the HET community. The declaration of separation may be found in an article by Margaret Schabas[1] published in the *History of Political Economy* in 1992 and titled, "Breaking Away: History of Economics as History of Science". This notion was supported by E. Roy Weintraub, also a past president of the History of Economics Society who is Professor in the History of Economics at Duke University, where the largest and most comprehensive graduate program in HET is found.[2] Here he sets out the nature of the

[1] Schabas is not, it might be noted, an economist first and foremost. This is from her biography posted on her home university website at the University of British Columbia:

> "Margaret Schabas was appointed to UBC as Professor of Philosophy in 2001. From 2004–2009, she served as the Head of the Philosophy Department. ... In addition to her doctorate in the History and Philosophy of Science and Technology (Toronto 1983), she holds a Bachelor of Science in Music (oboe) and the Philosophy of Science (Indiana 1976), a Master's degree in the History and Philosophy of Science (Indiana 1977), and a Master's degree in Economics (Michigan 1985)." (http://faculty.arts.ubc.ca/mschabas/)

She was President-Elect of the North American History of Economics Society as this book was being written in 2013.

[2] There should be no mistaking his eminence in the study of the history of economics:

> Professor Weintraub's academic awards include the Best Monograph Prize from the European Society for the History of Economic Thought and the Joseph J. Spengler Prize for the Best Book in the History of Economics from the History

difficulties facing historians of economics and considers why remaining within departments of economics may be a poor strategy for the long term:

> The institutional challenge remains to find academic sites for programmatic activity in the history of economics, not merely places that individual scholars can "sit and write." The history of economics needs to locate academic sites in North America that can provide *more* support than do research departments of economics. Since a number of historians of economics have intellectual affinities to the science studies community broadly understood, that realization can lead to their evolving connection with a potentially more welcoming scholarly community. But historians of economics will have to earn that welcome, since for example many historians consider work in the history of economics under-researched and over-interpreted, while many philosophers believe that too much work in "methodology" is insufficiently nuanced. Training in economics after all prepares one to do economics, not history or philosophy or sociology or anthropology or cultural studies. But early economics training can be an interesting base from which new skills, prized by other communities, can develop. And it is this kind of renewal that holds out some possibility of a more positive institutional future for scholarship in the history of economics. (Weintraub 2007: 279–80)

Much here depends on what the history of economic thought is intended to be a study of. If one undertakes work in HET, who would the intended readers of such research be? Or looking at it another way, who would read studies in the history of economics and for what purpose? From the perspective of the individual scholar the possibilities are open ended and may be different for each individual historian of economics. But I am not looking at the motivations of the scholar but at the nature of the study, what it is for and why it should be preserved. Crucially, the role of an understanding of the history of economics is to make economists better economists and to make economic theory even better than it is. It is to improve the study of economic theory by adding depth

---

of Economics Society, which were both received in 2005. He is a former President of the History of Economics Society, and currently he is Associate Editor of the History of Political Economy and the Economics Bulletin. In 2011 he was named a Distinguished Fellow of the History of Economics Society. (Bowmaker 2012)

and breadth. If you begin from the premise that the history of economic thought makes no difference to the science itself, that it has no beneficial effects on economists or economic theory, then by all means remove history of economics to anywhere you like. If that were true, it would make no difference where it was studied since so far as economic theory was concerned, it would be generally pointless anyway. If it makes no contribution to the collective understanding of economic issues, then the suggestion that HET be relocated to the history and philosophy of science would be perfectly sound.

A better appreciation of just how inappropriate this proposal is can be understood by looking at Schabas's 1992 "Breaking Away" article. What seems clear is that she sees no particular value for economists in having historians of economics within their faculties, attending their conferences or discussing economic issues with them where the economics of the past is brought into the conversation. She seems to have tacitly adopted the economics-as-physics approach where the economics of the past is just a compendium of dead ideas of no contemporary relevance. From there, she seems to have slid into the view that the study of economic history should be specifically designed not to rock the mainstream boat.

She does not see the history of economics in the same way as do many in the mainstream, that is, that it is a study with consequences because it provides alternative perspectives on economic theory. She does not see it as an integral part of the study of economics. She follows Weintraub in her concern that a "training in economics after all prepares one to do economics, not history or philosophy or sociology or anthropology or cultural studies", which are seen as deficiencies in converting HET into the history of science. Yet the problem with her approach is that in spite of being called the history of economic thought, it is not a study of history nor is it philosophy, sociology, anthropology or cultural studies. It is part of the study of economics and it can be done by no group other than economists and its findings are generally of no interest to anyone else other than economists.

BREAKING AWAY

At the very start of her paper Schabas notes the undisguised lack of interest in the history of economics by historians of science which is almost entirely matched by a mutual lack of interest by specialists in the history of economics in the history of science. There are some studies along both lines of inquiry but they are few in number relative to the larger interest in HET subjects by specialists in the history of economic thought whose discipline area is economics. And this is largely because no one ever looks at any of the traditional areas of research in the history of science with an eye on the relevance of this research to contemporary economic theory and policy. Things are different with economics, which frequently maintains its interest because of the theories held and conclusions reached by the economists under study.

A historian of science looking at physics, chemistry, medicine or any other area is somewhat detached from the science itself and is trying to answer a more sociological question. Those who look at the history of economics as often as not find themselves looking at quite profound answers to the very same economic questions being raised in their own time. It is why so many branches of the heterodox community find HET of such interest. They are looking at earlier incarnations of the very ideas they are trying to develop with the aim of learning something valuable themselves.

Schabas recognises the lack of interest amongst HET specialists in history of science type questions. But possibly because that is what does interest her, she misses what is right before her. In discussing historians of science, she notes that "as social historians, they now and again stumble over an economic fact or two, while suppressing recognition of the need to learn any economic theory" (Schabas 1992: 195). It is precisely that which is of no interest to a specialist in the history of science that differentiates someone interested in the history of economics, who is almost invariably also interested in economic questions and their associated theory. She asks, "why do historians of economics still attempt to speak to economists first and foremost?" (ibid.: 196). The answer is that only other economists will share their interests and concerns and will moreover be far more likely to understand what they are trying to say.

And many economists, even if they do not undertake such studies themselves and do not think it necessarily worth a semester of student time, do nevertheless value the history of economic thought. There is an audience of informed economists for the work that historians of economics do. Why would economists wish to join and seek a refuge amongst the kinds of scholars Schabas describes:

> As undergraduates, most historians of science either bypassed a study of economics altogether or were exposed to it in only its must rudimentary form. As a result, many are unfamiliar with the explanatory breadth and conceptual coherence of neoclassical economics *and tend to display the same disdain for economics as do their counterparts in the hard sciences*. (Ibid.: 195; my italics)

Given such "disdain" it ought to be little wonder that there has been so little attempt by historians of economics to make their way amongst historians of science. But it remains more than that since the questions the two groups are trying to answer are so different. Historians of science are talking about the sociology of knowledge. Historians of economics might sometimes talk about such matters but for the most part are interested in the different theories that have been developed to explain economic phenomena.

There is little likelihood that historians of economics as a group would agree to shift their home from departments of economics and become historians of science. But there is the possibility that those in leadership positions may agree to such a shift, which would cause long-term damage to HET but which they believe would actually be in the best long-term interests of historians of economics. As discussed in the next chapter, attempts to cause such a shift took place, first in Australia and then in Europe. The removal of the history of economic thought from within schools of economics is not an idle threat.

AN INSTRUCTIVE CORRESPONDENCE

There was an instructive correspondence on the history of economic thought website dealing with the role and significance of HET within economic theory that may provide an appreciation of how the history of economic thought is viewed by many within the profession. The correspondence in many ways underscores why the arguments found in this volume are different from those that might be found elsewhere. What that correspondence highlighted was the very different views of the role and significance of the history of economic thought held within the discipline by specialists in the area. And what made this correspondence so significant was that two of the most influential members of the history of economics community joined in the debate and gave their own views on the role they believe HET ought to play.

In drawing attention to this correspondence I wish to emphasise that I am not suggesting that there is no merit in the arguments presented by others. I have a clear preference for a particular view and for particular outcomes, which is why this book has been written. But there are other points of view worth considering which is the reason it is discussed.

The correspondence was initiated by a posting of my own on 13 March 2009. This was in the early stages of the global financial crisis when the level of economic uncertainty was at its most intense. The following is my original posting, lightly edited only to remove references to my own work. It was posted because *The Economist* was at the time running an on-line debate about whether a Keynesian stimulus package would make economic sense given the difficulties that the world's economy was in. What I found worth noting was that part of the discussion took up the issue of Say's Law and therefore explicitly dealt with an issue well within the realm of the history of economic thought. Or so I believed.

In understanding the following correspondence, it should also be noted that I had co-authored the opening article of a symposium on the role of the history of economic thought within economics, which was published in the July 2008 issue of *History of Economic Ideas*.[3] The symposium is almost unique as a site for discourse on the importance of HET in the development of economic theory and policy. This paper had itself evolved from an earlier experience in 2007 during which the Australian Bureau of Statistics had attempted to remove HET from the "Economics" classification within our national statistical collection and place it within a new

---

[3] My co-author was the President of the History of Economic Thought Society of Australia, Alex Millmow.

grouping which had been provisionally named, “History, Archaeology, Religion and Philosophy”. The effect of this re-classification, as benign as it may sound to some, would have effectively ended the study of HET within Australia since it would no longer have been considered a component of economics. The entire story is covered in the next chapter. Because of this background, I wrote the following post to the SHOE (Societies for the History of Economics) website.[4]

Original Posting

Many may have noticed that *The Economist* is running an online debate over the proposition, ‘we are all Keynesians now’. This is only a small part of an intense ongoing international controversy about the role of stimulus packages in the current economic environment. I think all of this is something that ought to be of interest to historians of economic thought for a variety of reasons.

(1) Brad DeLong is taking the affirmative side in this on-line debate. And in making his case, he wrote about the views of those economists who were opposed to the fiscal stimulus, and chose as his examples William Poole, Robert Barro, John Cochrane, Edward Prescott and Eugene Fama. These economists, DeLong wrote, were following Say’s Law. About their arguments, he wrote:

> ‘The argument that Messrs Fama, Prescott, Cochrane, Barro, Poole and company are making is what economists call Say’s law. It is the claim that decisions to increase spending – whether they come from the government or anybody else – cannot spur the economy and raise employment and production because demand must be created by supply. If the government spends, somebody else must cut back on their spending.’

This is, properly in my view, to plunge this debate on what policies to follow in the world’s economies at this time into the very depths of the history of economic thought.

(2) Economic theory has lost its ability to offer sound policy guidance because of the disappearance of Say’s Law. Many on

---

[4] The entire correspondence that followed from this original posting may be found on the SHOE website at https://listserv.yorku.ca/cgi-bin/wa?A1=ind0903d&L=shoe which includes my original posting.

this website will have seen previous postings of mine on this issue, but until now they were of only 'academic' interest. They are now matters of the most urgent public importance. Keynes never refuted Say's Law in any genuine way and the models he inspired have been notoriously wrong in providing advice to policy makers. Economists chose to follow Keynes, but not because he had demonstrated that classical principles were wrong or because Keynes's theories had brought the Great Depression to an end.

(3) The history of economics for economic theory generally is crucially important. Historians of economics, possibly because they have been shunned for so long, have retreated towards simply thinking of themselves as engaged in an arcane study of the history and philosophy of science with no real world relevance. This is positively wrong. Brad DeLong, even though he cites what he refers to as Say's Law, fundamentally misunderstands what classical economists had written and therefore cannot understand what classical economists were trying to argue. It is no wonder that he thinks we should still be following Keynesian prescriptions even as these very policies are leading the economies of the world into very troubled waters. Because he can see this as well as anyone else, he retreats to writing that 'even though Say's law is not true in general, could it possibly be true in this particular case?' How many questions does this then raise? Such a statement is a very very long way from a robust defence of Keynesian theory and a major step back towards classical economic thought.

(4) The history of economics is a necessary part of economics. Trying to flounder around with our present economic problems without having the ability to mine the theories of the cycle that existed before the publication of the *General Theory* means we as economists do not have the intellectual resources to think broadly enough about our current economic problems. This ought to be a time for historians of economics to remind their more mainstream colleagues why HET is essential to the study of economics proper.

First Roy Weintraub Posting

This posting brought forward a number of responses, but the following from Roy Weintraub was highly significant. Professor Weintraub is a former President of the History of Economics Society in the United States and Associate Editor of the *History of*

Political Economy. He is Professor of Economics at Duke University specialising in the history of economic thought. And on 25 March he wrote the following brief post:

> I'm confused. What does this have to do with the history of economics? Why would an historian of science care about which kind of reserve requirement is "best"?
>
> E. Roy Weintraub

Reply to First Roy Weintraub Posting

This brought directly into focus the issue that was central to my original posting. From the perspective of Professor Weintraub, economic policy questions are of no concern to historians of economics when acting as historians of economics. This was beyond whether a historian of economics would have any additional insights to contribute to such a debate. This was whether a specialist historian of economics should even care about economic policy. I replied to Professor Weintraub on the same day:

> Roy Weintraub has asked:
>
> > "I'm confused. What does this have to do with the history of economics? Why would an historian of science care about which kind of reserve requirement is 'best'?"
>
> Interestingly, this takes this discussion back to the original point I was trying to make which is the role of HET in contemporary debates. The mainstream thinks there is no role for HET in the development of economic theory and policy, but that we have known for a long time. But what Roy's question does is essentially agree with the mainstream but in the reverse direction, by asking what role does a discussion of contemporary issues have in HET?
>
> My answer is that HET has a very great deal to offer as this quite interesting and high level series of postings has shown. There are many ideas embedded in historical discussions of economic issues that are relevant in the current economic climate that the mainstream would have no access to but for the efforts of historians of economics. And what I feel is worse, for the most part the mainstream would not even think of looking in this direction for guidance. This is where they need to be educated by us.
>
> Just to go back to the debate that took place on *The Economist* website, there were over 300 replies, and in spite of the specific

reference to Say's Law by Brad DeLong (good for him), only three of the subsequent postings made any reference to what really ought to be one of the main areas of interest in trying to think through whether Keynesian theory gives us any assistance in dealing with our present economic problems.

HET is part of economics proper or it is part of the history and philosophy of science. I think it is the first. If, however, trying to use HET to think about modern economic problems is not part and parcel of what specialists in HET would be expected to do, then we really ought to just pack up shop right now.

Steve Medema Reply

I was not alone in taking a similar position, but the reply from Steve Medema was addressed to my own posting. Medema was the editor of the *Journal of the History of Economic Thought* from 1998 to 2008 and was not only on the executive committee but was also President-elect of the History of Economics Society in the United States at the time he wrote the following on 27 March:

> I would suggest that there are elements of good sense in both sides of this discussion, but also problematic bits. The history of economics has plenty to say about the present economic situation; in fact, I spent 90 minutes last night talking to a room full of scientists about exactly this. There are also several papers that will be presented at this year's HES conference that bear on this subject. An understanding of the history of ideas is of no less import for dealing with the present than is understanding the history of events. That said, there are several problems with the position taken by Kates. (I use him as an example because of the pithy statements he offers.)
>
>> "HET is part of economics proper or it is part of the history and philosophy of science. I think it is the first."
>
> Why is this an either/or? I would think that it could very well be both. In fact, I DO think that it is both.
>
>> "If, however, trying to use HET to think about modern economic problems is not part and parcel of what specialists in HET would be expected to do, then we really ought to just pack up shop right now."
>
> "Part and parcel"? That means, an essential or integral component of what an historian of economics/economic thought does. This would deny that it is legitimate to study the history of economic thought for its own sake, as a branch of intellectual history or the history of science. I

simply cannot accept so narrow a definition of the legitimate province of the historian of economics.

There is also a certain amount of hubris in the statement, re. mainstream economists, that "This is where they need to be educated by us," but the problems go beyond that. Too often history of economic thought takes the form of trying to use the past to show contemporary economists they are wrong. That is perfectly legitimate as a form of scholarship, but I question whether it is scholarship in the history of economic thought. It USES the history of economic thought, but it does not necessarily contribute to (and often does not contribute to) our understanding of the history of economic thought. And all of this is apart from the fact that the context in which these writers of the past wrote – the import of which is shown in HET as intellectual history/ history of science – is often very far removed from present economic problems.

The distinction here is really between studying the history of ideas and disciplines vs. using that history toward a particular end – whether it be to prop up what passes as the mainstream at any given point in time, or to attack it (or the equivalent on the policy front). There are obviously plenty within our tribe who fall into each camp, and some who fall into both. A third way is to use the ideas of the past to help us understand the present – without passing judgment. The group working in that arena is much smaller. I have great sympathy for the first and third of these approaches, but not so much for the second. I will stop short of suggesting what, among these things, appropriately belongs in JHET [*Journal of the History of Economic Thought*], HOPE [*History of Political Economy*], EJHET [*European Journal of the History of Economic Thought*], etc. That is for editors and referees to judge.

Steve Medema

Reply to Steve Medema Posting

There is a great deal of food for thought in Medema's posting. Of particular significance was his division of the uses that HET could be put to into three broad classifications:

1. studying the history of ideas and disciplines as just a thing in itself with no other motivation other than to know what had happened
2. using that history of ideas and disciplines toward a particular end – whether it be to prop up what passes as the mainstream at any given point in time, or to attack it

3. using the ideas of the past to help us understand the present – without passing judgement.

The first and third he has sympathy for, "not so much" as he put it for the second. Moreover, his advice to journal editors and referees was that articles with that second motivation have no place within journals specialising in the history of economic thought. My reply was sent on the same day.

> I am very grateful for Steve Medema's comments because it will help me clarify what I was saying. And indeed, he himself states that "the history of economics has plenty to say about the present economic situation". There is almost no limit to how true I think that statement is. That is why I replied as I did to the suggestion that a discussion which invoked the history of ideas to deal with contemporary economic matters is not only part of the history of economic thought but is in fact part of the study of economics itself.
>
> It may well be that my close involvement with the attempt to reclassify HET out of existence here in Australia has made me more than normally sensitive to these issues. What has happened here in Australia can happen anywhere. That is why I believe that we as historians of economics need to understand the role of HET within economics if this sub-discipline of ours is to survive. Just how little appreciation there was, at first, for the role of HET within economics was quite astonishing. For it to have reached the point it had when we historians of economics finally became involved required almost the entire official world of the social sciences community to have already signed off on the reclassification.
>
> The existential issue for us was whether HET is economics or whether it is instead the history and philosophy of science. Yes, it is both, but in which of the two does it make its way in the world? In my view, it is the first of these two and it is only for that reason that HET is an essential component of economics itself.
>
> In my view it is not an overstatement to suggest that specialists in HET would be expected to think about modern economic problems. We are economists and economists do think about economic problems, and we use our specialist knowledge to reach conclusions that would often be different from the conclusion reached by someone starting from a mainstream economics position. Not all students of HET think about contemporary economic problems, of course, but then again, not even all economists do so either.
>
> The approach to the history of economic thought that Steve has the least sympathy with is "using that history toward a particular end," that is, either using HET to support the mainstream or to attack it. Well,

perhaps I would put it this way, that this is using HET to help economists understand economic issues and to guide economic theory towards a better explanation of how economies work with the final aim of improving economic policy.

If this is not a significant part of what HET tries to do, then the Australian Bureau of Statistics was right, and HET should be reclassified as part of the history and philosophy of science and HET specialists should move out of economic departments where most of us are now found. But I don't believe that nor does Steve. You do not become a better physicist by reading Newton, Rutherford and Einstein, but you do become a better economist by reading Adam Smith, Marx and Hayek.

In this, I do not suggest what the motivations behind the work of individual scholars ought to be. What I was writing about is the role of HET itself apart and separate from the individuals who till its fields. In the HEI symposium, there were many ideas worth considering, but amongst them was something written by Sam Bostaph (I hope he forgives me for dragging him into this). This was summarised in our symposium rejoinder:

> "[Bostaph] rightly states, 'anyone who is conducting a research program in economic theory cannot avoid the necessity of drawing upon past intellectual history'. Research into the history of economics, he notes, is a form of specialisation and division of labour. If economists are to have access to the 'history of doctrines, methods, analysis, definitions and controversies' that are necessary inputs into their own work in theoretical and applied economics, there has to have been a prior effort amongst historians of economics to make this work accessible."

This is a form of the invisible hand. We each please ourselves with our own work for whatever reasons, but even so each of us may well be promoting ends that were no part of our original intention.

For myself, I find HET endlessly fascinating. On my office shelf I have only a single book from my days as an undergraduate these more than forty years ago, and that single book is Mark Blaug's incomparable *Economic Theory in Retrospect*. It is a work of such astonishing scholarship that even then I knew it set a standard I could never hope to reach.

I took to HET not because it can be used to repair bad economic theory, but because I loved the history and evolution of ideas. My stumbling across Say's Law came decades later. Steve however asks whether we should use the past to show contemporary economists they are wrong. He writes that this is "perfectly legitimate as a form of scholarship, but I question whether it is scholarship in the history of economic thought."

Well, my view is pretty clear on this. Using the past is, in my view, not only a very important part of contemporary economic debates, but is also part of what historians of economics do, and an important part. HET journals should not, of course, be used to discuss economic policy issues; that is not what they are for. But discussions amongst historians of economics are where economists clarify amongst themselves those ideas which have descended to us from the past. Perhaps, as Steve suggests, the history of economic thought is not the place for such discussion. But if not here, where? and if not us, who?

Second Roy Weintraub Posting

This reply of mine to Steve Medema led to a further response from Roy Weintraub. On 29 March he sent the following posting to the HES website:

> Steve Kates wrote:
>
> > You do not become a better physicist by reading Newton, Rutherford and Einstein, but you do become a better economist by reading Adam Smith, Marx and Hayek.
>
> This seems to be the issue. Who in fact is making the "better" determination? All Kates et al. seem to be saying is that "better" is defined by "having read canonical author X, where X is my boy Smith or Ricardo or Mill or Marx or George or Keynes or Hayek or …" If you are really an economist, I would have thought that you would have agreed that "better than" is a partial ordering relationship on the set of economists. And certainly that ordering is individualistic. Put another way, for those who have read Robbins but not Koopmans, interpersonal comparisons of utility are a big "no-no". So all I take from Kates and Gunning et al. is that most contemporary economists have different preferences from those that Kates et al. seem to share. This is no essentialist matter, to be decided by one true revelation of that which is, but rather it is a pragmatic matter of what works for a particular community as it pursues its own local and contingent objectives. And an overwhelming majority of modern economists find HET of no use whatsoever in their own projects. Attempting to valorize that belief, that choice, is simply a waste of time. It is akin to trying to convince Netanyahu that Palestinians have a right-of-return, or to convince the Indian Prime Minister that Kashmir is part of Pakistan. Good luck.
>
> E. Roy Weintraub

Reply to Second Roy Weintraub Posting

My reply to Professor Weintraub on 29 March closed off the correspondence on this topic.

> It is quite instructive to me to find that amongst historians of economics, it is in any serious way controversial to have written that, "you do not become a better physicist by reading Newton, Rutherford and Einstein, but you do become a better economist by reading Adam Smith, Marx and Hayek". And what I mean by "better" is straightforward enough to me: economists are more likely to add value in whatever projects they undertake if they have studied HET than if they have not. I cannot see how being ignorant of the history of the relevant theory leaves an economist on an equal plane with a second economist, equally well endowed with knowledge and technique but who has studied HET as well.
>
> I am more than content to accept that this is the central issue but if it is, then we are living in an entirely different moral universe. Whatever pre-postmodernism is, that is me. I do think some conditions of the world are better than others. I am judgmental about some things and this is one of them.
>
> If it is true [!], as Roy wrote, that "an overwhelming majority of modern economists find HET of no use whatsoever in their own projects" then this is either because they have knowledge of HET but this knowledge provides them with no useful insights (but how would we know this is true even if we thought it?), or they do not have any such knowledge and therefore cannot know one way or another whether such knowledge would be of any use to them if they did have it.
>
> Or to put it more bluntly, an understanding of HET is either useless to economists in their professional lives as economists or it is not. Roy seems to think it is useless, I do not.
>
> This is not something we will resolve here on this website, but it does seem to me to be the major issue in HET. Roy would, it seems to me, be fully content to join historians and philosophers of science and withdraw HET from the economics discipline. I not only do not want to withdraw from amongst economists, I want to stake out a position amongst mainstream economists that reminds them of just how valuable and important HET is to them.
>
> Economic theory without HET is a very thin and uninteresting area of study it seems to me. I can almost not think how economics can be done at any depth without HET but maybe it can. Maybe economics really is like physics (or dentistry) with its history of no use in the practice itself but it would then be a subject so shallow and superficial, that it would not be worth the effort.

But tell me then how to classify this. The first sentence in the first article in the October 2008 issue of the *Journal of Political Economy* (Vol 116 Number 5) reads as follows:

> "Becker's (1957) seminal *The Economics of Discrimination* launched the formal analysis of labor market discrimination amongst economists."

What the article does is test Becker's predictions. It is therefore mainstream economics but is it not also HET? There is no reason that that same sentence could not be the first sentence of an article found in HOPE or JHET. This is going into the past to go forward.

I don't know what economists in general believe about HET and its uses. But if they think everything they need to know can be found in the latest journals and the most recent texts, they could not be more clueless about the kinds of knowledge that might actually assist them in their work. That I actually find that most economists I know do appreciate HET and would like to have a deeper knowledge may only be a reflection of the different circles in which we travel. I am not prepared to retreat into the history and philosophy of science just yet, and if the profession at large has any idea what's good for them, they will make sure that doesn't happen either.

SOME COMMENTARY

We who study the history of economics approach our own researches with different motivations. One can study Adam Smith, say, for entirely historical reasons unrelated to contemporary policy issues. Or one might study Smith for historical reasons but suddenly find that the insights gained have a contemporary policy relevance. Or one might study Smith specifically because of the insights he might offer in regard to the economic issues of our time. One might even be interested in Smith for entirely philosophical reasons unrelated to any economic purpose whatsoever. The aim of the researcher is whatever it might be but is basically personal and has little to do with the subject itself.

However, one of the most important issues in a discussion of the role of the history of economic thought is to identify whether it has an important role to play within the development of economic theory and policy. To return to Professor Weintraub's question, "why would an historian of science care about which kind of reserve requirement is 'best'?" But supposing not a single historian of economics does care about any of this, the question still remains whether the research that HET specialists have undertaken into, let us say, the history of monetary theory, and their examinations of and writings on the works of monetary economists of the past has cast any light on more recent monetary and other aspects of economic policy.

Partly through contact with HET specialists, partly through personal research of their own, economists dealing with practical policy questions have their answers informed by studies that are undertaken into the history of economics. Economists who have studied the works of Thornton, Ricardo, Tooke and Fisher will have insights useful to others. Thinking about Fisher, it might well be asked whether studying Friedman today is part of modern economic theory or is part of the history of economics. When do the insights provided by an economist transfer into history and disappear from mainstream economic consideration?

Market economies do not change that much, nor are our problems all that different from the past. The complexities that the economists of the past were dealing with have not been resolved with modern economists moving onto a deeper level while the concerns of earlier times have been left behind. We are still grappling with the same sets of problems. Listening to others trying to come to terms with those same issues two centuries before we have tried to do the same increases our understanding. Their ideas may be useful just taken straight, they may be useful in helping us to frame our own answers or they may be useful in providing a platform to reach a higher level of comprehension. The mainstream of the profession at the moment is of the belief that investigating the views of earlier generations of economists provides them with less value than the cost of discovering what those economists had to say.

If this were the case, then there would be almost no value in HET being taught to economists other than as a form of ancestor worship. Nor would it much matter whether it was taught and studied by economists within economics departments or was, instead, taught as the philosophy of science to students of cultural studies. But it is not the case, as Steven Medema's posting should make clear. To repeat, Medema argues that there are three possible reasons for studying HET:

1. studying the history of ideas and disciplines as just a thing in itself with no other motivation other than to know what had happened
2. using that history of ideas and disciplines toward a particular end – whether it be to prop up what passes as the mainstream at any given point in time, or to attack it
3. using the ideas of the past to help us understand the present – without passing judgement.

The first of these is what might be described as "the Weintraub approach". It is HET as a scholarly activity undertaken with no particular intent in mind other than a desire to know. This is a purists' version of the subject, and may indeed represent the approach of the majority of those engaged in HET. Most academics are not involved in policy questions. They pursue areas of interest to themselves for personal reasons which are largely of no extrinsic interest. Whether or not such individuals have economics training is irrelevant nor does it much matter who their readership is. It is a study undertaken only for its own interest with no wider concerns about relevance to the rest of the world. It is the classical picture of an academic and of an academic pursuit.

Medema believes that the Weintraub approach is completely valid as a direction for scholars of the history of economic thought to take but also accepts the third, "using the ideas of the past to help us understand the present – without passing judgement". Let us call this third possibility "the Medema approach" since this is what he has done himself in relation to the global financial crisis. As he wrote, "an understanding of the history of ideas is of no less import for dealing with the present than is understanding the history of events", but in providing such an understanding, one should not use the research one undertakes to attempt to pick and choose between different policy directions. So far as policy is concerned, when undertaking research into the history of economics one should remain agnostic; one should not pass judgement on the policy choices made by governments and other decision-making bodies based on these studies.

To use the previous example, one might become a scholar in banking policy, know the entire literature from 1750 until 1900, have written extensively on this issue and the views of all of the great economists, then discover that a major topic of political and economic debate is the reserve requirements of banks but decide that one should not do any more than place the facts before others and let them reach their own conclusions for themselves. One might even present a conference paper at a conference on the history of economic thought discussing these issues but even then no judgements should be passed.

There is then the second possibility listed above, which I will call "the Adam Smith approach" following Smith's use of economic history in the *Wealth of Nations*, where he contrasted his own theories with the mercantilist doctrine of Thomas Mun, who had written more than a century earlier.[5]

What I take from the distinction made by Medema between his own approach and the Adam Smith approach is that if one follows the Medema approach, one should not then use the knowledge one has gained in studying this area in the history of economics to undertake research on these issues within the context of the history of economic thought nor should one apply any of the conclusions reached to form a judgement about policy. Because such an economist is shifting into that second category, "using that history of ideas and disciplines toward a particular end – whether it be to prop up what passes as the mainstream at any given point in time, or to attack it." It is this option that Medema has little sympathy for. This is not, in his view, what scholars in HET really ought to be doing.

Such discipline seems not only superhuman but decidedly pointless. If someone has a comparative advantage in a particular issue which they have gained through mastery of an area of economic scholarship, the community loses the value of what that scholar has discovered. But because such self-discipline would seldom if ever be exercised by scholars with a depth of knowledge in an area of public debate who are also able to find their way into the public square should they so desire, it is not likely to lead to a loss of policy advice. To the extent that it did, it would be a net loss to society.

But in reality, the question is not whether individual scholars within HET should be involved in discussing public issues using

---

[5] The relationship between Thomas Mun and Adam Smith was discussed in Chapter 2.

their knowledge of the history of economics. It is whether they should use the platforms provided by HET journals and conferences to discuss contemporary issues.

But even more to the point is this. The core issue is whether the subject area of the history of economic thought adds to the study of economics. The question is not whether there are a thousand other uses for HET, but whether the subject area of economic theory and economic policy are diminished without the history of economic thought being an integral part of it. This is the only issue that matters, and neither Professor Weintraub nor Professor Medema have even begun to deal with this as the core issue.

What drives the research into HET is irrelevant to recognising that such research is an important component of the study of economics itself. Economic theory and policy development require that the study of the history of economic thought takes place side by side with the other core areas of the curriculum. The uses that are made of the research into HET are separate and apart from the research itself. My issue is not with what historians of economics do but with what economists do. Historians of economics are merely the means by which policymakers and their economic advisers come into contact with historic ideas beyond the mainstream. That is why I wrote:

> "You do not become a better physicist by reading Newton, Rutherford and Einstein, but you do become a better economist by reading Adam Smith, Marx and Hayek."

As I read Weintraub's reply, my understanding is that there is no point in arguing from authority about any of the economic issues that divide us. Since one can only argue from one's own perspective, in going back to earlier generations of economists all one is doing is finding a genealogy for one's present beliefs. As far as he is concerned, HET should not be the feedstock of ideas for contemporary debates, with the most important reason being that if you do not believe some argument in the first place, having an ancient economist quoted at you will make no difference.

This enters quite deep currents of epistemological truth. But if one accepted his conclusion, it would lead to a complete abandonment of any and every attempt to discuss economic issues with someone else. Bringing Thornton, Ricardo, Tooke or Fisher to the discussion may not win an argument purely on weight of authority. But if their arguments are sound, or if their arguments can be developed in ways that capture important aspects of an issue, their contributions can be valuable. Such grounds for belief will, of course, seldom be decisive but the sound good sense of so much of the economics written in the past does help to clarify issues before us in the present.

In his conclusion, Weintraub adds that "an overwhelming majority of modern economists find HET of no use whatsoever in their own projects". But even if most, at present, find no direct use for past theory in their economic work, even on Weintraub's assessment some clearly do, and all benefit from living amongst a pool of economists some of whom are well versed in the history of their subject. The aim amongst historians of economics – not all but at least for some – is to remind the mainstream of the profession that there are valuable insights to be found amongst our forebears. And while it may be that there will never come a time when the majority of economists make any use whatsoever of the economists of the past, it is in their interests to ensure that those economists and their ideas remain alive within the economics communities in which they work. The result is a deeper, richer tradition upon which they can draw, even if they themselves are only reading the most recent papers or the latest texts.

SUMMARISING THE DEBATE

In summary, what is presented in the present work is different from the view presented by those who see HET more as history of science than a relevant strand of economics, and therefore as entirely separate from on-going debates about theory and policy. It is also different from the view of those who believe that the history of economic thought should be designed so as not to create ripples on the mainstream pond. The argument of this book is that the history of economics is economics and that one of its roles ought to be seen as confronting economists in the present with arguments made by economists in the past. It may be, as some suggest, largely unconvincing and a waste of time. There may be no point in expressing these views to other historians of economics within journals devoted to the subject since those who drive theoretical change and policy development seldom pay serious attention to debates amongst historians of economics. Anyone wishing to convince economists of some point of view may find this not to be the playing field they should be on. Leave history of economics journals for scholarship about the history of economics and engage with other economists about theory in journals that are devoted to theory may well be the right approach.

Yet, even while most of what those who would prefer a more ascetic view of the history of economic thought may be correct, there are reasons to see things differently, that there is value in using HET in more general theoretical debates within economics. Many of those who study the history of economics develop ideas based on the thinking of the economists whose work they have examined. If someone believes that there are arguments found in Wicksell, let us say, that are relevant in managing a modern economy, the first staging post on the road to influencing the profession is to discuss what one has discovered with others who have studied and understand Wicksell's work. Such people will for the most part be historians of economics. And while the number who do have such knowledge will be relatively small, there will be some. The first port of call for serious review and debate is within such specialist journals. Where else can it be done? Who else will do it?

The academic journals of economics, especially at the higher end, are almost entirely devoted to mathematical and statistical treatments of economic issues. If the aim is to focus attention on some historic argument that may have relevance in a contemporary setting, debates amongst historians of economic thought, and even within HET journals, ought to be seen as worth encouraging. The history of economics ought to be thought of as an avenue for bringing ideas into the mainstream conversation.

Below is a summary of the arguments presented. They outline in half a dozen points the perspective presented in the book:

- economists looked at individually have a stronger grasp of economic theory and therefore make better economists if they have studied the history of economic thought,
- economics as a discipline looked at as a collective enterprise is much improved by the existence and work of such historians of economics,

- economic theory is improved by the work of historians of economics who are able to bring insights from the work of economists of the past into the current conversation,
- economic theory is improved if economists generally actively look amongst the work of economists of the past for a theoretical understanding of contemporary issues,
- it improves the skills and abilities of the community of economists as economists if they collectively and individually have a greater understanding of economic theory's past and the different perspectives it provides,
- the history of economics as a subject area must remain part of economic theory, recognised as such by both economists and the official classification agencies of government.

The work of Adam Smith, just to take one example, would be completely inaccessible if it required an individual economist to read *The Wealth of Nations* from cover to cover to find out what Smith had said, what he had meant and why it was significant. We never think twice about how immediate the name Adam Smith is to an economist. We do not see it as remarkable that economists are at least to some degree familiar with even those small parts of what he wrote that they are aware of. But without historians of economics, Smith and his work might be as well known to economists in general as the works of James Steuart or Nassau Senior. The secondary literature points scholars towards the primary sources which historians of economics are continuously expanding. But because individual economists have this knowledge, economists collectively have this knowledge. And even where economists on an individual basis do not personally have this knowledge, other economists with whom they associate may have such knowledge and in reviewing their work or discussing some issue will bring this knowledge into play either explicitly or indirectly.

Thus whatever else may happen, at the end of some research into the history of economics, such scholars will have a sharper understanding of economics than they previously did as will those who engage with their writings. Such research will make the study of economics more interesting and add to the collective wisdom of the economics community. None of that may be the intention of any individual scholar but that will nonetheless be the effect. It will also have other forms of influence beyond economic theory and to others who do not participate in the economist's craft. That is, of course, a positive externality but one which is not part of my concern in this book.

4. Teaching the history of economic thought

> No branch of philosophical doctrine, indeed, can be fairly investigated or apprehended apart from its history. All our systems of politics, morals and metaphysics would be different if we knew exactly how they grew up, and what transformations they have undergone; if we knew, in short, the true history of human ideas.
>
> (T.E. Cliffe Leslie 1888: 22)

There would be no particular point in teaching economists the history of economic thought if it did not make them better economists. Which raises the question, what makes someone an economist at all? Is one an economist if one attempts to answer economic questions regardless of qualifications or technique? Is someone an economist if they attempt to answer economic questions no matter what qualifications they might actually have or which analytical techniques they might happen to use? Or is there a body of theory that unifies this diverse group of individuals under the common name of "economist" whether or not they possess any particular technical abilities? And if there is such knowledge required, is some educational institution required to certify that someone has that knowledge if they are to be officially classified as an economist? And if someone is a certified economist, what should someone else, an employer let us say, or perhaps another economist, expect that person to know or to be able to do?

Here is my answer. An economist is someone who understands modern textbook economic theory, can apply that theory to answer questions about the economy and has graduated in economics from some tertiary institution where their stock in trade is the theory they have learned. If they know only technique, then they are not economists in any interesting sense of the word. An economist is someone who knows economic theory and in the modern world has a university degree that establishes the possession of such knowledge. Conversely, whether a university graduate or not, anyone who does not know economic theory cannot be classified as an economist.[1]

At the very core of the education of an economist are microeconomic and macroeconomic theory. No matter what other areas an economist might choose to specialise in, this is what they will know. No university teaches only a single micro and macro course to anyone it intends to certify as an economist but will teach each of these subjects at least twice, where there is greater detail, further elaboration and usually a more mathematical treatment provided as the student progresses through the syllabus. Virtually every graduate course in economics will also teach micro and macro and where PhD comprehensive exams are given, virtually every economist will be expected to pass their micro and macro once again.

So here is the point. What makes someone an economist is their knowledge of economic theory. Learning the history of economic thought makes an economist a better economic theorist. And if properly taught, the difference is not just incremental but will make a major difference to an economist's abilities. Therefore, to become better economists, students of economics should be instructed in the history of economic thought.

The opportunity cost of time spent with HET is time lost on some other area of study that might have been more valuable. In an era where mathematical and statistical technique is taking precedence over theoretical underpinnings, the question becomes whether having learned the history of economic thought will add more value to the array of abilities that the economist can bring to the issues that will need to be dealt with later on. There are, perhaps some career paths for which additional maths and stats may be more beneficial, but for most economists who must deal with policy issues and then communicate their conclusions to those who have not formally studied economic theory, the benefits in studying HET will outweigh the benefits of additional courses in technique. And while this may not always be the case, it will be the case in a very

---

[1] There are, interestingly, courses that teach merely econometric techniques separate and apart from formal theories in economics. Students in these courses are not economists in my view, although their skills would be quite useful in a range of applications.

large number of careers, and probably in the majority. Here is a short list of how learning HET makes one a better economist:

- it makes an economist better at thinking about theoretical issues in the abstract
- it gets past the routine of what is taught in the first year that is amplified in later years and instead provides a parallax view that a different perspective provides
- it emphasises that there are other ways of thinking about issues that economists in the past have found fruitful
- it deepens intellectual judgement in general
- it deepens an economist's understanding of existing theory by making them look at economics when other perspectives were dominant
- it broadens an economist's understanding of existing theory by taking them back to the origins of these concepts when they were fresh and contested
- it develops the ability to turn economic conclusions into words that can be used to explain one's own conclusions to others who do not have a background in economic theory
- it develops the ability to assess economic facts and ideas
- it fosters historical thinking as a routine means of looking at issues
- it develops the ability to read with meaning
- it heightens an economist's ability to write
- it encourages economists to look for answers amongst the theories that were developed in earlier times
- it develops critical thinking since economists will need to think through for themselves why present theoretical understanding is superior to the understanding of economists in the past
- it emphasises the logical connections between aspects of reality
- it is a reminder that running regression lines through incomplete and flawed data sets may not be the perfect way to do economic analysis and is certainly not the only way
- it makes the study of economics far more interesting.

The narrowness of the current teaching of economic theory at undergraduate level is quite astonishing. A range of largely identical introductory texts supplemented by similar texts in later years that rehearse the same set of theories but using more advanced techniques is how everyone now learns the subject. More advanced classes include journal articles – which are almost invariably highly mathematical – that attempt to demonstrate some conclusion but in which textbook economic theory itself plays a minor part at best. The challenge of different ideas, the true life of scholarship, is almost invariably diminished. And I would emphasise this: that if learning the history of economics doesn't interest you then economics itself doesn't really interest you. If the history of economics doesn't interest you, then you should perhaps find some other area of study.

ECONOMICS WILL NEVER BE A SETTLED SCIENCE

Everything you read in an economics text was once controversial. In fact, just about everything you read in an economics text is still controversial, and this will be as true as far into the future as you care to go as it is today. That is what the history of economic thought is for. It is to introduce students to the great controversies of the past and to demonstrate how relevant those same discussions and debates remain.

Economics is not physics. A modern physics text is up to date in the important sense that it is complete in and of itself. Concepts and theories once superseded never return. No idea of consequence falls out of discussion. No questions asked by physicists disappear because the physical environment has thrown up different questions. A physics book of twenty years ago or more is positively misleading, if not actually wrong. The study of the history of the natural sciences is unlikely to make someone a better physicist, that is, one who is better able to answer contemporary questions.

Economics on the other hand is almost entirely the reverse. Past economic concepts and theories do inform current debates. Economic theory consists of perspectives on how to analyse economic events that can never be demonstrated as valid to the same degree as in the natural sciences since every event in the world comes with a different set of surrounding circumstances. Major issues come and go, so that what is of interest in one era may have no interest at a later date and fall out of textbook treatments. Most importantly, an economics text of a century before, rather than being filled with discussion of no interest in the present, will instead contain insights into economic processes that will appear fresh and interesting to someone who has never read outside a modern text or recent journals. The potential for an economist to be stimulated by such reading is high, with a consequent deepening of their ability to think like economists.

Moreover, in physics, unlike any of the social sciences, the scientific method of repeatable experimentation is at the very heart of theoretical development. In the social sciences there are few ways in which to test and demonstrate conclusively that one view of the world is better than another. We may have more data at our disposal and we may have more in-depth mathematical techniques and computers to run our models on, but at the very centre remains the need for a coherent theory on which to base the maths and the modelling. What ends up in our texts are the survivors of a process in which truth and accuracy are the aims but in which propositions must run the gauntlet of a mass of philosophical, political and social filters before finding their way into a standard textbook discussion.

HOW HET IS TAUGHT

The typical way in which HET is taught is by assuming that the present textbook treatment is not just the outcome of the most recent attempts to make sense of the confused events of the world but that it is the correct perspective at long last laid bare and revealed. The assumption that underlies most treatments of HET is that all previous attempts to make sense of the operation of the economy were the fruits of a primitive comprehension of the actual relationships involved which has evolved into the more complete understanding we have today. This may be the best way to teach economics since the classroom, especially at the introductory level, is not necessarily the place to open different perspectives on these various issues. When teaching theory, the aim is to pass on to others the latest answers to the complex problems thrown up by economic activity. Even where some historical perspective is offered, it might well be acceptable to assume that the latest textbook answer is, if not the "right" answer, the best answer available at the present time.

And that, of course, gets us much closer to the issue. Textbooks provide answers but they often leave out the questions. Ignored are the circumstances of the time, the problems that were being dealt with when the theories were being formulated and the various alternative perspectives that were offered up in their stead when those theories were developed. What is left is the residue of some earlier debate at some earlier moment when a particular set of circumstances led to a certain set of conclusions which became solidified in the textbooks of the time and which have been bequeathed to us in the present.

But while in teaching economics and economic theory the role of history has only a limited place, there does need to be within the core curriculum of every student of economics a place where greater attention is given to older ideas and to the roads along which the development of theory proceeded. And while the tendency might be to provide a few historical examples within the structure of a course – along the lines of the thumbnail sketches provided by Samuelson in his archetypal text – something more is needed as part of the serious education of an economist, and this is as urgent at the undergraduate level as at the graduate level. And what is needed is an understanding of the theories that are taught embedded in the story of how those theories arose in the first place.

The difficulty that plagues most of the approaches to the history of economics is that we teach the subject as a sequence of ideas that followed one upon the other. First there was this economist and this is what he taught and then there was that economist and this is what she taught and so on and so on, with each economic theory seen to have replaced the one before in a piecemeal sort of way. In the meantime, a poor student is asked to come to terms with a sequence of theories, each as complex as the ones found in a modern textbook but prefigured with the admonition that the theory is wrong and has been anyway superseded. It is a history of ideas with much of what is of interest and importance left out.

Just as economic theory today is being forged in response to current economic events and explanations, so too were the economic theories of the past derived in the same way and in response to particular circumstances. There were events taking place and explanations made for what was taking place, usually with an aim not just to understand but to shape events in a more appropriate way. Understanding why *The Wealth of Nations* was written in the way that it was and published at the time it was published requires someone to understand, at least in part, the changes taking place in the economy of late eighteenth-century Britain and the content of contemporary political debates. These were the early days of the industrial revolution, there had been a change in both the politics and the political philosophy of the era, there were others writing on economic issues, and there were a series of policies that Smith had in mind on how to improve various aspects of economic management as they were then practised. To stay with the example of *The Wealth of Nations*, as most students of HET are aware, what was seen to be important in the book also changes with time and circumstance, with the metaphor of the "invisible hand" of virtually no interest during the first century after the book's publication but now seen as of crucial importance. Indeed, for the majority of economists this now constitutes almost the whole of the meaning of the thousand pages of text.

Just knowing this should awaken the interest of any student of economics with even the slightest pretence to a philosophical soul – a character trait of supreme importance if one is to become a serious economist with genuine depth. Knowing the results of a regression is often interesting, but to understand that economics is a philosophical study of humans in relation to their material wellbeing, and the means by which material wellbeing is achieved and improved, is more important still. That regression or mathematical model must sit within some context. And the context is not another regression or mathematical model but society, made up of living human beings, in which the economy itself, with all of its various structures and relationships, is an entity buried within an actual existing political community in which the discussion of economic issues may or may not take place. Without that understanding, economics is soulless and of less practical value than it might otherwise be.

The history of economics is therefore about controversy and conflict. It is about the clash of ideas. It is about the meeting of the human equivalent of tectonic plates where those with different perspectives have tried to convince each other that their own view of the world is the correct one. It is not just a study of first-there-was-this-and-then-there-was-that. It is not just a sequential study of the order in which particular ideas came to dominate the mainstream only to be supplanted by other ideas which took their place. Too much of the history of economic thought has been taught along those lines, in much the same way that biologists talk about the evolution of the horse.

That deprives economics of much of what is not only interesting but also relevant. There is at any moment a standard accepted theoretical consensus view on each of the main elements not only of what is within economic theory, but even of what constitutes the subject matter of economics. Over time these change, partly because new answers become accepted and partly because the events of the world bring into the foreground other questions that require investigation while older answers appear increasingly inadequate. It is these changes that ought to be the substance of the teaching of the history of economic thought.

Therefore, in discussing what should be taught it might be worth emphasising what should not be taught. The teaching of the history of economics to students of economic theory is not about the details of the subject. It is not about teaching the kinds of discussion found in a modern specialist journal in the history of economics, no more than an introductory course in economics should be focused on what may be found in the latest economic journals.[2] In the case of both graduates and undergraduates the history of economic thought needs to be taught in such a way that the broad sweep of historical development is understood and the great questions of the past are made comprehensible. The broad aim is to sit modern economics within the context of the economics of the past and, importantly, to have students appreciate that almost every aspect of the theory they are learning as the most modern and up-to-date will, in time, become part of the study of the history of the subject.

A journal devoted to the history of economics would therefore seldom be the source material for students. Journal articles typically delve deeply into a very narrow part of some historical issue that would be of limited interest even to most specialists, never mind a wider and less informed audience. It would be without purpose and

---

[2] Blaug (2001: 147) points out how the academic study of the history of economic thought is flourishing while the teaching of the subject is falling away. I suggest that these are two almost entirely different constituencies with only a limited overlap in terms of purpose and interest.

sense to ask an undergraduate student of HET to read or understand any such material. That is for later in life when they may or may not have developed a deeper interest in the study of the history of economics for themselves.

WHAT YOU SHOULD WANT A STUDENT TO KNOW

If I were to construct an ideal history of economics course, the curriculum would be focused around an examination of a succession of basic textbooks from their earliest manifestation through to the most recent textbooks used to teach undergraduates today. Start wherever you like, perhaps with an investigation of the first textbook treatments currently available in a cheap edition and then move forward in something like quarter- or even half-century lots. A progression might look like the list offered below, but these are listed only as examples and others could easily be preferred. And let this be stressed: no course would teach anything like all of the books listed but would focus on three or four texts spread perhaps fifty years apart. Moreover, one would not go through any of the books entirely but would focus on two or three topics and look at their treatment in the three or four texts being used for comparison within the course. But once the book is in a student's hands, their own curiosity could be expected to induce further exploration of the text. I have chosen the following examples because most have variations on "principles of political economy" as part of the title. I have included the year of first publication below, but these will seldom be the easiest editions to find. The bibliography lists the editions that I have used myself.

1825: J.R. McCulloch: *The Principles of Political Economy*
1848: John Stuart Mill: *Principles of Political Economy*
1871: William Stanley Jevons: *Theory of Political Economy*
1890: Alfred Marshall: *Principles of Economics*
1911: Frederick Manville Taylor: *Principles of Economics*
1911: F.W. Taussig: *Principles of Economics*
1940: Lewis A. Froman: *Principles of Economics*
1948: Paul Samuelson: *Economics: An Introductory Analysis*

1960: Campbell McConnell: *Elementary Economics: Principles, Problems, and Policies*
1988: William J. Baumol: *Economics: Principles and Policy*
1998: Gregory Mankiw: *Principles of Economics*

It would be notable that in the half century between Mill in 1848 and Alfred Marshall in 1890 there is a chasm between what is taught and how, whereas in the half century between the first editions of Samuelson in 1948 and Mankiw in 1998 there is a gentle evolution with comparatively little to separate the concerns of the two periods. Many of the more recent changes are merely related to the technology of the publishing industry, including the ability to reproduce graphs and charts in full colour. But the difference between Mill and Marshall is the advent of the marginal revolution and between Marshall and Samuelson there is the Keynesian revolution. Since then there has been a remarkable stability in as much as it would be somewhat archaic but not entirely beyond the realms of possibility to use Samuelson (1948) in a classroom today.

Having said that, there are of course very different kinds of material found in a modern text that would not have been found in the earliest Samuelson, including additions such as aggregate demand and supply curves, behavioural economics and the economics of the environment. But in reality, not all that much has changed since the end of the 1940s.

AN EXAMPLE FROM THE PAST – MONOPOLY

There are many possible examples that might be used to show how microeconomic theory has developed, but the one chosen here is the treatment of monopoly. Discussion of monopoly has remained virtually unchanged since the 1940s but the presentation in modern texts is very different from examples that might be plucked from the more distant past. The basis for textbook presentations at the present time is a combination of Chamberlain's *Theory of Monopolistic Competition* and Joan Robinson's *Economics of Imperfect Competition*, both published in 1933. Their analyses and the accompanying diagrams are now the staple of every microeconomics course taught round the world. But you really do wonder whether quite a bit of insight has been lost in the transformation from a reasoned discussion into an abstract set of diagrams.

Begin with John Stuart Mill's *Principles*. In his "Summary of the Theory of Value" he more or less summarises the issues in a single sentence:

> A monopoly value means a scarcity value. Monopoly cannot give a value to anything except through a limitation of the supply. (Mill [1871] 1921: 478–9)

In this one sentence we find much that could be gleaned from the standard diagram. This is a statement based on Mill's earlier discussion in his chapter on "Demand and Supply". There he wrote:

> There are but few commodities which are naturally and necessarily limited in supply. But any commodity whatever may be artificially so. Any commodity may be the subject of a monopoly: like tea, in this country, up to 1834; tobacco in France, opium in British India, at present [1848]. The price of a monopolized commodity is commonly supposed to be arbitrary; depending on the will of the monopolist, and limited only … by the buyer's extreme estimate of its worth to himself. This is in one sense true, but forms no exception, nevertheless, to the dependence of the value on supply and demand. The monopolist can fix the value as high as he pleases, short of what the consumer either could not or would not pay; but he can only do so by limiting the supply. The Dutch East India Company obtained a monopoly price for the produce of the Spice Islands, but to do so they were obliged, in good seasons, to destroy a portion of the crop. Had they persisted in selling all that they produced, they must have forced a market by reducing the price, so low, perhaps, that they would have received for the larger quantity a less total return than for the smaller: at least they showed that such was their opinion by destroying the surplus. … Monopoly value, therefore, does not depend on any peculiar principle, but is a mere variety of the ordinary case of demand and supply. (Mill [1871] 1921: 448–9)

This is different in texture from the standard treatment found in a modern text. It points out that if a seller can restrict supply and make it stick then the price charged will be higher. A supplier will also aim to locate the price in the elastic part of the demand curve. But it embeds the concept within supply and demand analysis and looks at the practical side of the issue. Turn then to F.M. Taylor's 1925 exposition of the same issue. The discussion of monopoly is found in his chapter on "Special Cases of Normal Supply" (Taylor

1925: 342–56) in Section V, "Price Under Monopoly". Taylor here follows Mill in seeing monopoly as a subset of the study of supply and demand:

> Price-determination under monopoly is not a process entirely different from those already described, but merely a variant from them. Monopoly, as it were, injects into the situation a new condition under which the principles already noted as operative work out the result.
>
> The first point to be made is that, in respect to its one immediate determination of price, we have under monopoly merely a special case of fixed-supply goods. The supply of the monopolized good is a fixed one; but this fixedness is not of natural origin, is not due to any absolute limit nor to the limit of our capacity to produce. Rather, the monopolist consciously, arbitrarily, limits the amount produced, or, at any rate, the amount put on the market. (Taylor, ibid.: 351)

Taylor then follows with a principle followed by a corollary followed by a second principle which takes the concepts surrounding monopoly to a different level. This is Taylor's first principle:

> **Principle.** Broadly speaking, the normal price of any monopolized commodity tends to be that price which will secure the largest net return to the monopolist. (Ibid.: 353)

Diagrammatically, there is a precision as we now teach the theory that is absent here. In this older version there is an in-built recognition that these are mere tendencies in which a monopolist is thinking strategically about what can be done to increase revenue to the greatest extent. Taylor then goes on to discuss the effect of elasticity on revenue which makes finding the right price that much more difficult.

> **Corollary.** The tendency of a monopoly price to rise above the competitive normal varies inversely as the elasticity of the demand for the monopolised commodity. (Ibid.)

Taylor notes in the text that this has implications for the behaviour of the seller in dealing with the market situation. He points out that "the appearance on the market of a commodity which can be used as a *substitute* for some monopolized one diminishes our dependence on the latter and so makes its demand schedule more elastic" (ibid.). Taylor then discusses what he terms "capitalistic monopolies" which occur when there are huge start-up and capital costs involved in the production of some goods. But even then, such monopolists must keep looking over their shoulders to make sure they are not overtaken by a rival. This is the second principle he therefore derives:

> **Principle.** The normal price of goods produced by capitalistic monopolists tends to approximate a figure not much above costs of production to outsiders. (ibid.: 354)

This is different from the way in which we now commonly discuss the issue in terms of marginal cost and marginal revenue, which teach and explain the actions of a monopolist as though it were a mere technicality in finding the profit maximising point. We use *MR* = *MC* to provide an answer to what the price will be but have no genuine idea how they could ever be calculated or any actual evidence that most firms use such a technique other than as a summary of the ultimate objective in the abstract. We offer a false precision that may have little actual relevance to price determination at the firm level.

Froman (1940) moves the argument substantially towards the present and includes an extended discussion along the lines of *AR*, *MR* and *MC* as it is typically found today. But it is a transitional text so when he comes to discuss monopoly (471–98) he begins by noting that "it is difficult to formulate a definition of monopoly which is useful for all occasions", a welcome recognition of an ambiguity seldom found today. But he again explains the concept in a way that is fully in accord with Mill:

> A seller's monopoly may be defined as a seller or a group of sellers who, by restricting production, can bring about price changes to their advantage. (Ibid.: 471)

He then goes on, mirroring Taylor:

> Perhaps the most important aspect of monopoly activity (certainly the most talked of) is the price which is set by the monopoly. Does the mere existence of a monopoly necessarily mean that any price may be charged? Between limits which may be considered as "reasonable" this may be true, but it does not necessarily follow that a monopoly will

> charge the highest price that it can get away with. A monopoly will set its price *at that point which will yield the greatest net revenue*. It is important to observe at the very outset that this "point" is not necessarily a high price. (Ibid.: 476)

Froman then provides a numerical example to emphasise that the price will be crafted with a range of considerations in mind. The conclusion reached is far different from the kinds of static analysis we commonly teach today. The following kind of observation does not follow from equating *MR* and *MC* in the standard monopoly model.

> Monopoly price in our illustration definitely is not the highest price which it is possible for the monopoly to charge. On the other hand, it is one of the lowest of the prices which have been assumed to be within the range or probability. … If our example is representative of costs and prices, it will permit the generalization that the reduced cost resulting from a greater production may induce a monopoly to choose a larger production at a lower price instead of a smaller production at a higher price.
>
> As previously indicated, the primary purpose of a (sellers') monopoly is to be able so to control supply as to affect price advantageously, and, the most advantageous price is that which yields the monopolists the greatest net returns. Just how far the monopolist should go in the curtailment of output or how high he shall set the price to achieve maximum net profits will depend upon a variety of factors. (Ibid.: 477–8)

Compare this analysis in which the price depends on "a variety of factors" with the structure of the argument today. At these earlier dates, imprecision was the key. No one knew anything for sure and there were many considerations that had to be taken into account. Even if we recognise that these considerations exist, which we seldom do as we introduce economic students to monopoly and market structures in general, the nature of the analysis is built around the design structure and analysis illustrated in Figure 4.1.

It is possible that at the end of quite a bit of hard work, a student will master the diagram and what it is intended to show. And when all is finally said and done, the conclusion a student would be asked to accept would be that there is a single price at which a monopolist will aim and there is a single volume that will be sold. The effort involved in coming to terms with the diagram inhibits the inclusion

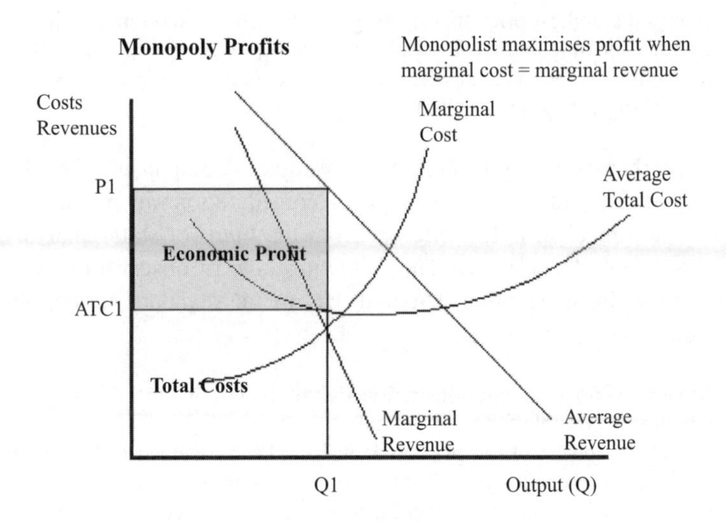

Figure 4.1 Monopoly under marginal analysis

of further considerations. But what is worse, once the diagram makes sense, it is this that becomes the way in which virtually any economist who considers monopoly looks at any associated questions and the policy framework. Whether this is the best way of looking at the question of monopoly is not the point. What I am trying to do is to stir a recognition that there were once other ways of looking at monopoly that did not start with this framework but instead thought about the issues in a variety of ways that were different from how they are thought about now. The older form of analysis may appear more vague, less precise than our modern analysis does to modern eyes but it also does not assume knowledge on behalf of decision-makers that they could not possibly have. They understood price setting was a trial and error process with considerations about the present and future balanced against each other. Could the same be said of an economics student today, given the way in which they are taught?

What studying the history of economic thought ought to be able to do is to draw the attention of economists to these alternative and now discarded approaches to looking at various issues. It would not be surprising to find that economists, once they had come to understand the standard apparatus used today, would prefer it to the looser, less deterministic approach of these earlier times. But even if they did, they would still have seen that there are different approaches that have been used in the past that embed this concept in a different surrounding context and from which different conclusions may be reached. This is knowledge in itself.

But it is also possible that some students will have learned something valuable about the nature of monopoly that they would not have discovered had they been confined to modern textbook treatments. At the very minimum they might become open to different ways of thinking about monopoly. They might also become aware that there are other – potentially fruitful – ways of thinking about this issue. Experience with monopoly might encourage them to extend their range of inquiry when examining other topics.

Further, it would take a student deeper into economic theory since it would open the entire history of the subject as a valid potential store of concepts and ideas that could have relevance in their own work. It would change the dynamic of economic thinking if such historic views were routinely sought; in teaching modern economic theory, having the past as a context will add an important dimension to the flat textbook discussion. The contrast between these two ways of discussing much the same complex of ideas would engage the more serious students and could not fail to enlighten even those who find the modern standard discussion clear and comprehensible. By bringing in this contrast with an alternative approach that had not been discredited but rather superseded by the graphical approach of the 1930s, something is learned about the nature of monopoly at the same time that something is learned about the nature of economic theory. The history of economics comes alive, as does the subject of monopoly, and by extension this could be applied to the entire modern approach taken to what is called "the theory of the firm". An economist who has studied and thought about this older tradition is a better economist for having made the effort.

A SECOND EXAMPLE FROM THE PAST – THE BUSINESS CYCLE

Turning from micro to macro, almost parallel with the shift in the analysis of industry structure has been the shift in the way in which economists look at the nature of recession and unemployment. Today's macroeconomics was formerly referred to as the theory of the business cycle and, unlike monopoly where it is possible to see a direct evolutionary relationship, the connections between macro-economics and the theory of the business cycle are almost non-existent and in many ways contradictory, both in regard to the causes of recession and the steps that might usefully be taken to mitigate their effects.

And it is not irrelevant to point out that the basic approach to macroeconomics and variations in the level of economic activity and therefore variations in the level of employment centres around the Keynesian notion of aggregate demand, summarised and explained in every textbook within a format that discusses these issues in terms of $Y = C + I + G$. Whatever direction a student's education takes thereafter, reaching even into graduate work in economics, there is seldom any formal severing of what is taught from the aggregate demand framework introduced to all students in their first course in economic principles. And why that has continued to matter is how that very little bit of the history of economics is taught when dealing with the Keynesian revolution. It was Keynes who argued that his classical predecessors had no theory of recession. In a famous and very influential passage in *The General Theory* Keynes wrote:

> The aggregate demand price of output as a whole is equal to its aggregate supply price for all volumes of output, is equivalent to the proposition that *there is no obstacle to full employment*. If, however, this is not the true law relating the aggregate demand and supply functions, there is a vitally important chapter of economic theory which remains to be written and without which all discussions concerning the volume of aggregate employment are futile. (Keynes 1936: 26; emphasis added)

Keynes's statement that so far as classical theory was concerned there is no obstacle to full employment in any model of the economy that had previously been devised became, and largely remains, the accepted belief about economists before 1936. Here is Greg Mankiw in the fourth edition of his *Principles of Economics*, published in 2007, stating why the economic theories of Keynes's predecessors could not be employed to analyse the cycle:

> Do those assumptions of classical macroeconomic theory apply to the world in which we live? The answer to this question is of central importance to understanding how the economy works. *Most economists believe that classical theory describes the world in the long run but not in the short run. …*
>
> To understand how the economy works in the short run, we need a new model. This new model can be built using many of the tools we developed in previous chapters, but it must abandon the classical dichotomy and the neutrality of money. We can no longer separate our analysis of real variables such as output and employment from the analysis of nominal variables such as money and the price level. Our new model focuses on how real and nominal variables interact. (Mankiw 2007: 744)

A student would therefore believe, as Mankiw himself must apparently believe, that economists prior to Keynes had developed no theories of recession, did not even try to make sense of short-term fluctuations in the level of output or employment, blandly assumed that money was neutral so that variations in the supply of money were irrelevant to the nature of the economy, and that the real and monetary economies – the classical dichotomy – were never discussed at one and the same time. This is the tradition that every economist has been brought up to believe however wrong it may actually be.

There are therefore at least two matters that should be understood as of some urgency for economists. There is, firstly, an imperative that the record be set straight. It is a considerable problem when economists are actively taught that the great economists of the past were vacuous ciphers, not only with no insight into the nature of recession but unable even to recognise that this was the case. We have taught generations of economists something so monstrous that if it were true it would not have been beyond the bounds of sense to have wrapped the entire economics enterprise up and given it all away. But it is not true and the most astonishing part is that it is known to be untrue. The definitive article was written early in their careers by two giants within economics, one now associated with the free market side of economic analysis and the other a Keynesian but also himself very much an advocate of free market solutions to our economic problems. In an article by Gary Becker and William Baumol published in 1952, they addressed the question of whether the accusations made against classical monetary theory were correct and came to a very clear answer which they stated right at the start.

> It will be argued through re-examination of some of the classical writings that most of the group probably never held views like those ascribed to them. … Many of the members of that group, among them some of those specifically accused, have passages in their writings which explicitly contradict the charges against them. … In most of the cases where the problem was considered *explicitly*, it was analysed in a manner which is at least formally valid. (Becker and Baumol 1952: 355–6)

It is probably, however, safe to say that virtually no one reads these classical writers now, so what they said is a closed door to almost the entire profession. Not one economist in a hundred (a thousand?) could discuss any of the monetary theories of the nineteenth century and that might even include Mankiw himself. But why that is important in this instance is not because there is value in what they wrote, although there is, but because the general misapprehension of the past is part of the reason that economists think there would be no value in examining the theories of the cycle that had existed before the publication of *The General Theory*.

This, then, is the second matter. Not only do we need to set the record straight about the competence and depth of thought of economists before Keynes, but it is imperative that economists are re-introduced to the theory of the business cycle which had been developing for over a century before its existence was for all practical purposes eliminated from the study of economics right across the subject. It is simply a fact that virtually no living economist has any idea of the body of work that was encompassed within the theory of the cycle that had developed since the beginning of the industrial revolution in the mid-eighteenth century, a period that saw the very first cyclical downturns in Europe, a phenomenon that had never been experienced before.

By the end of the nineteenth century, because the business cycle was such a prominent and dominant part of the experience of everyone who was then living within industrialised economies, business cycle theory was a recognised aspect in the training of economists who tried to make sense of what was to them a common phenomenon. Is it remotely plausible that anyone would have accepted an answer along the lines of, don't worry, it will all blow over in a few years? But what answers economists had constructed, and there were many, are to economists today a virtual unknown, thanks to the mischaracterisations that began with Keynes. And the tacit assumption is that there is nothing there to investigate, nothing we can learn today from their experience then and the conclusions they drew in the middle of recessions that were in most essentials no different from the ones we experience today.

The point at which to begin a review of the classical theory of the cycle is with a book published in 1937. The book, *Prosperity and Depression* by Gottfried Haberler, was written following a resolution of the League of Nations in 1930 which "decided that an attempt should be made to co-ordinate the analytical work then being done on the problem of the recurrence of periods of economic depression" (Haberler 1937: iii). The aim of the publication was stated in the introduction:

> The purpose of the first part of this report – *i.e.*, of the Systematic Analysis of the Theories of the Cycle – is not to present a history of the development of economic thought on this subject … nor to give anything like an exhaustive bibliography of business-cycle theory. The purpose is rather to gather together various hypotheses of explanation, to test their logical consistency and their compatibility with one another and with accepted economic principles. It is intended to give a rounded picture of the possible explanations of economic fluctuations and it is hoped that, by theoretical reasoning, the numbers of these possibilities can be considerably reduced. (Haberler 1937: 1)

There, within a single set of covers, was Haberler's attempt to explain the theory of the cycle as it had developed to that point, which was just as *The General Theory* was published, for all practical purposes obliterating the study of the cycle from the curriculum of economists. Although the term itself has survived, along with the rhythmic chart showing the contours of the cycle from peak to trough, the accompanying theory has gone. And while virtually no one any longer knows classical business cycle theory, how likely is it that there is nothing amongst all the theories that had been discussed by economists for almost two centuries that would provide insights into the problems of the modern world? No one who has not looked into these earlier theories with a proper spirit of inquiry can give a negative answer to this question. Not because they have investigated these earlier theories and found them wanting, but because they have never investigated these theories at all.

But supposing that modern theory really is better in every way. Even then, would it not benefit a student of economics to think about economic issues through the eyes of classical business cycle theory? Would there not be value in a consideration of these various issues from the different perspectives of some of the most insightful observers of economic activity who have ever lived? These were the people whose views dominated their own times. Is it not possible that their ways of thinking have something to contribute to ours? That is the question a proper history of economic thought should attempt to answer. And at the very least, attempting to explain why modern forms of analysis are better would be a useful challenge for a student thinking about economic issues in general.

WHAT IS PROPOSED

The most important aspect of this proposal is that students in the history of economic thought are not to be guided through the economics of earlier times through texts written at some later date that try to explain to modern readers what these earlier economists had said. This proposal is different. It argues that students should go to original sources – not necessarily to the various landmark papers and texts that changed the nature of economic theory, but rather to the economic textbooks that were used at the time.

Take the two examples I have provided, the change in the discussion of monopoly which is now dominated by the $MR = MC$ diagram and the emergence of Keynesian macroeconomics which has as its own equation the $Y = C + I + G$, which are the components of aggregate demand. Both developments occurred in the 1930s. A typical HET course, if these events were discussed, would mention Joan Robinson and Edward Chamberlain in the first instance and Keynes in the second. A course might then ask students to look at Joan Robinson's *Economics of Imperfect Competition* or Keynes's *General Theory* and would comment on the change as seen from today's perspective. And in both instances, because what would be at the core of the description would be the supplanting of an older view with the modern, the necessary implication would almost inevitably be a form of Whig history where the superior had replaced an inferior form of theoretical discussion. Embodied in such instruction would therefore immediately be a prejudice that what is being learned is inferior, and aside from the necessity of passing an exam in the course that it would really have no further value or interest to a student in thinking about economic issues.

In contrast, the suggested approach ensures that what is being examined is not a second-hand account written by an economist at some later date and from a different era looking back with full knowledge of which side will prevail in debates that were not even in the wind when these books were written, but is, instead, an actual discussion by someone writing at the time who is trying to explain a particular point of view in as logical and persuasive a way as possible. Just as we cannot know what economic theory will be like fifty or a hundred years from now, so these textbook writers of the past could not know what economic theory would be like today. They described the economic world as well as they could and applied the theory they found most applicable to conditions as they understood them.

And this is economics, not physics. There are no undiscovered fundamental particles within economies or unknown forms of motivation or new discoveries about human nature. We have technologies and information sources that were not available in the past, and we can do in-depth computations with data sets that were unimaginable in earlier times. But when it comes down to the basic theoretical models and the way the world can be conceptually organised, there is truly nothing new under the sun. A textbook from a century ago will therefore not be some foreign territory entirely filled with conceptions difficult to grasp and requiring clarification through the acquisition of additional background information. There are, of course, issues that have disappeared, such as the controversy over bimetallism. But for the most part, the meaning of these earlier texts will be readily apparent. And in going through this material, a student would not only be learning the history of economics but would also be acquainting themselves with ideas that will be of use in understanding modern theoretical structures through the capability of seeing them within the context of earlier theoretical structures.

And as hard as modern writers on the history of economics might try, they can never fully re-capture the past because they do not fully accept either the arguments or the theories. They will inevitably outline these theories in straw-man versions, certain that they are to be knocked down by our more accurate, more recent versions. If they thought the earlier modes of instruction or theories were superior, they would teach those instead. Inclusion in this way of these older economists and their theories in a course in HET introduces a necessary condescension. This is what they believed but they did not have the benefit of learning from the great economists who came after so their economic theories are therefore primitive versions of what we know today if not actually completely wrong. By going to the original sources, the past is given the opportunity to speak for itself as clearly as possible and in its own voice.

Moreover, the books referred to should be the mainstream texts of the time, not the antecedents of the various heterodox traditions that exist today. This is not a criticism of non-mainstream positions. It is only stated to ensure that the focus of such studies into the history of economics is on what the economists of that earlier mainstream had once generally accepted. There are always, in every generation, different perspectives that are alive to a minority of those who work in the economics field. On occasion such heterodox views do become the mainstream, as when marginal analysis replaced the classical theory of value. Jevons notoriously taught Mill, while despising the economics he was compelled to teach. To teach in one of the heterodox traditions and provide a history of ideas may be a legitimate approach but it is not what is being advocated here. This proposal is specifically focused on providing instruction in the introductory economics that was taught to all young economists when they were first introduced to the economic theory of a bygone era.

For example, Marx and his views would not fit into a history of economic thought syllabus as it is here conceived. The case for teaching the economics of Marx is weak since so little of what was contained in Marx entered mainstream theory and therefore virtually nothing that was discussed by Marx has ever been explicitly included within mainstream economics proper. The point being made here is that economic theory has a history that is now almost totally ignored, the mainstream theorists of the past are names almost without serious content and almost no economist today would be familiar with the work of the mainstream of the economics profession before the 1930s and possibly for a good deal of time after that. Marxist economic theory was never part of the mainstream outside of communist countries and therefore belongs to a totally different tradition. Marxist economics should therefore not be taught in a history of economics class other than as a curiosity.

And I would say the same about what is now described as "Austrian Economics", although there is a greater justification for teaching much of what is in that tradition since a good deal is an intrinsic part of the mainstream. Nevertheless, much of what may be thought of as within the Böhm-Bawerk/Weber/Mises/Hayek tradition was not included in the standard textbook tradition. For those who teach from an Austrian perspective (as with those who might teach with Marx at the centre of their core syllabus) using the traditional teaching of economics as the basis for teaching the history of economics allows this different approach to be seen in the context of a different genealogical descent.

All economists should recognise that there is a common core tradition in economics; and it is that which should constitute the history of economic thought so far as it is taught to all students of economics. There can also be the history of Marxist economics, the history of the Austrian School, the history of institutional economics, the history of post-Keynesian thought or any other part of the heterodox tradition. But every student should know the common core of contemporary economics and its history. These should be common ground for every economist.

TEXTBOOK QUESTIONS AND ANSWERS

Beyond the text itself, the value of placing the emphasis on contemporary textbooks of the past lies in the opportunity to understand the motivations of the writer through examining the questions that were included for students to answer. When this practice arose is an unknown but it was common by the start of the twentieth century and unknown at the start of the nineteenth. But in between the practice grew up of asking questions as part of the way in which economic theory was taught and learned.

The questions were therefore an integral part of the learning process. They were designed to help mould the students' ways of thinking so that they understood both the kinds of issues the theories were designed to explain and the kinds of answers that were understood to move towards an adequate response. The Q&A became an integral part of the instruction.

But the same would be true for a present-day student of the history of economics. Some of the questions are no longer relevant because they refer to issues that have not survived the passage of time. Questions on the gold standard, for example, may have some value in causing students to think about problems in the abstract but since exchange rates are no longer based on a gold equivalent and no government tries to keep the value of its currency within some pre-determined range, there is no contemporary relevance for such questions and little would be learned by thinking such issues through. This is not to dismiss these questions as entirely unimportant, but if we are trying to demonstrate to students that there were questions in the past that are as relevant today as they were on the day they were formulated, then not all questions from earlier texts should be seen as equal in value.

The questions below come from Fred Manville Taylor's 1913 edition of his *Principles of Economics*. They are placed at the end of chapters on particular topics in order to test what the student has learned. They are not particularly difficult questions but might require quite a bit of thought for a student who had not come across the problem before. They are also useful in promoting thinking through important economic issues. First this, which follows the chapter on "Mechanisms of Exchange".

> We buy a good deal from Brazil, but sell her little. We sell a great deal to Great Britain, but buy from her much less. Can you imagine a way in which one of these trades furnishes a medium of exchange for the other? (Taylor [1913] 2008: 139)

This question is from a chapter dealing with "Final Price Determination".

> Some writers are accustomed to speak as if the value of each particular kind of goods were determined by *its own* marginal utility solely.
>
> Show that, even if it is to be admitted that utility is, ultimately speaking, the only cause affecting values, the position alluded to is after all quite untenable. (Ibid.: 300)

This third question would draw students (and I dare say their lecturers) into thinking about economic matters in a way that is today entirely foreign to their ways of understanding the operation of an economy. It might also be worth pointing out that Taylor was the author of the attempt to refute Mises in the socialist calculation debate (Taylor 1929) so he was in his time very much to the left of the political spectrum. Here is the question and it comes from his chapter on "System of Distribution" and is the kind of question any economist would have been expected to be able to answer.

> It is usual to say that even goods ready for consumption, e.g., a loaf of bread, are capital *so long as they are in the hands of the producers or dealers.*
>
> (a) Try to show that such a way of looking at the matter is reasonable.
> (b) Is there any interest present in such a case?
> (c) Can such capital properly be described as productive?" (Ibid.: 369)

For a modern student, it would not be whether such a way of looking at things would be reasonable but whether it would even be comprehensible. This question comes from a very different way of looking at not just the meaning of capital but also at the meaning of interest. In asking whether this loaf of bread is "productive", would a student today even understand what makes the question worth asking? In going back to Taylor and reading his chapter, a depth is added to the narrow frame of reference that students who know only their own textbook theory and our modern textbook ways of looking at issues would find difficult to make sense of and to provide an answer for. Graduate students would find themselves grappling with questions whose premises would be as unfamiliar to them as would the expected answers.

Would an economist be a better economist for having to deal with such questions, chosen almost at random and from a single text? It is no wonder that HET is on the wane when we march our students past empty questions such as the wages fund doctrine, pour scorn on these older ideas and teach them in such relentless detail that it is frequently beyond endurance. And at the end of the programme there are a few names that one can associate with the origins of a handful of ideas but there is very little real learning. In contrast, imagine a student made to read a few chapters in Taylor's eminently accessible text. It is in no sense archaic either in its ideas or its language. It is economics through and through. It summarises the views on economics that were prevalent in 1913. Students who read what Taylor wrote would be able to make sense of concepts that we now teach in such isolation from their fuller contexts that they become almost impossible to appreciate.

Think how much more deeply students of economics would understand the economics of their own time if they had gained a genuine understanding of the economics of earlier times and could demonstrate this by answering questions that had been formulated to accompany an earlier text. They are asked to consider old questions which they can answer using the economic framework of the text from which the questions are derived and the framework they have learned in their own core subjects in economics. It would be a very dull student of economics indeed who would not profit from the thought processes necessary to arrive at answers to these older questions from texts that may no longer be used in a modern principles course but which still have much to offer in terms of illuminating various issues from different points of view.

THE ROLE OF TRADITIONAL APPROACHES TO THE TEACHING OF HET

What, then, for the traditional teaching in the history of economic thought. There have been roughly three approaches. There is, firstly, the chronological approach, which considers the development of economic theory by looking at the various changes and additions that were made to the original ways of conceiving economic issues, perhaps going back to the physiocrats or Adam Smith. Here was the diamond–water paradox and then marginal utility was discovered and so Adam Smith's way of looking at the theory of value was replaced by a newer, better approach.

This is like looking at the evolution of the car from around 1903 by examining all of the parts that had been replaced over the years, working backwards from today to decide what has to be explained with regard to future development. We would go from the engine to the tyres to the roof to the pedals, looking closely at each development but at every moment being aware what the final automotive product would be. The early car, like early economic theory, would be presented as a primitive version of the modern with each of the changes along the way having been components in the improvement in the overall final product. So to continue this analogy, one might look at the crank that was once used to turn an engine over and then be shown the starter motor and discuss when and how this improvement had come about, all the time assuming a Whig history where the final product is the superior product in every detail (which with a car it is). But what you end up with in a car is a history of the componentry and the same is true of economics; the picture is not the actual conceptual structure of economics at different moments in time which ideally we would be trying to teach.

The history of the development of different aspects of economics is the second approach and it is even more abstract than the first, which is at least embedded within some kind of fuller context. This second approach looks at the history of individual concepts, such as the history of the theory of value or the history of the theory of the firm. This is even more disjointed than the typical chronological sequence which has advantages in allowing a focus to be placed on how conceptual ideas were developed over time in relation to each other. It can be allied in the car analogy with the history of ignition, which almost entirely abandons discussion of the rest of the car in its focus on the single conceptualised product that exists in the present.

Then there is a third approach, which is to discuss economics through the development of different competing schools of thought, often called the history of doctrine. This is not quite a parallel approach since to some extent they deal with succession as the typical run from classical, through marginalist and then onto neo-classical which often incorporates Keynesian macroeconomics in its compass and sway. This approach is typically used so that other non-traditional approaches can be brought into the narrative.

Each of these approaches would not only be consistent with the methodology outlined above but would also be essential if the history of economics was to be grasped in full. This is particularly the case with the approach that looks at the sequential development of economic thought. To return for the last time to the car analogy, we would start with the most primitive engine, the economics of the classics as exemplified by some early nineteenth-century text. Between its publication and the publication of John Stuart Mill's *Principles* there would have been a number of changes made to the exposition of economic theory – among them major controversies such as Malthus's theory of population and the general glut debate. There would also have been various events that would have influenced the development of theory, such as the first major cyclical downturns ever experienced by an industrial nation, which would also have been accompanied by significant increases in national and personal wealth. Thus by the time John Stuart Mill's *Principles* was published, it was a different world, into which new ideas would have been interwoven, partly because of historical events and partly because of the broad acceptance of new ideas.

The interest, therefore, is in the theory at two points in time and the ways in which the theory had developed. The nature of the evolution of theory would therefore be one element in such a course, but just as important would be the role of new ideas and historical events, which would be occurring in the present just as they occurred in the past. To help students to understand the ways in which ideas come and go and the ways in which specific events that weigh heavily on the minds of theorists affect the theories they develop would be an important element in the education of economists. Again, this is theory that unlike the natural sciences is powerfully affected by contemporary events. To choose the most obvious example, it is unimaginable that *The General Theory* could have been written at any time other than in the midst of a major economic downturn – nor would it have had the impact that it did if it had been written by someone without Keynes's reputation and literary skill.

The material in a traditional HET text would therefore tend to come alive in ways that traditional teaching does not encourage. Rather than it being a succession of ideas one following another without an appreciation of the framework in which those individual ideas subsist, there would first be a framework established consisting of the general economic approach of the time as found within a typical and standard text. At this stage, and as found in most history of economic theory courses and texts, there would be a discussion of the ideas that had been developed by various leading theorists. It is here that the traditional text would be introduced as part of the exposition of the ideas themselves. This would be followed by a discussion of a later economics text to show how these new ideas were embedded in the way economic theory was then taught to all.

Traditional HET would therefore be prefaced by an appreciation of the theory that had previously existed and then followed by a discussion of how the new set of ideas was incorporated into the surrounding text. Although in one way it could be said that there is an even greater burden placed on students since they would be required to come to terms with not just the new theoretical development but also the old and new frameworks, the reality is that the additional learning required would make the traditional HET more comprehensible, not less, and more interesting, not less.

An element not found in traditional HET teaching would have been added. And what would have been added is the full context of the change involved. New concepts would be seen as being brought into an existing body of theory which must itself change to make room for the new theoretical structure. Economic theory would be seen as recognisably organic, growing and accommodating itself to new ideas. It would make the history of economics come alive while making students exposed to the evolution of these ideas better economists.

CONCEPTS AND DIAGRAMS

Amongst the most momentous changes in the manner in which economics has been taught, which is unmistakable from an examination of textbooks written before and after World War II, is the proliferation of diagrams. The argument in earlier texts was carried in the words and not in the manipulation of lines on a graph. Even in Marshall's discussion of "Equilibrium of Normal Demand and Supply" in the *Principles*, the supply and demand curves are only shown a single time and found in a footnote (Marshall [1920] 1947:

346n). Students were asked to apply logic and reason in understanding the underlying economic relations. In a modern text, there is an apparatus presented that one learns to manipulate and the shifts in diagrams need to be interpreted in order to understand that the equilibrium price and volume will necessarily have shifted.

The diagram gives a kind of precision to the underlying reality that just may not be there.[3] A modern text will tend to present a kind of stability in equilibrium different from the kind of message Marshall was trying to convey.

> The demand and supply schedules do not in practice remain unchanged for a long time together, but are constantly being changed; and every change in them alters the equilibrium amount and the equilibrium price, and thus gives new positions to the centres about which the amount and the price tend to oscillate. …
>
> We cannot foresee the future perfectly. The unexpected may happen; and the existing tendencies may be modified before they have had time to accomplish what appears now to be their full and complete work. The fact that the general conditions of life are not stationary is the source of many of the difficulties that are met with in applying economic doctrines to practical problems. (Marshall [1920] 1947: 346–7)

This is qualitatively different from the way supply and demand is normally taught today where an equilibrium exists until it is disturbed by some shift in *ceteris paribus* conditions. Marshall is discussing an ephemeral momentary focal point that may be gone in a moment. He immediately goes on to discuss the need to understand that there is no stability in the equilibrium he has described. He concludes in a way that would seldom be discussed in a modern text but which may nevertheless be entirely valid.

> Thus we may conclude that, as a general rule, the shorter the period which we are considering, the greater must be the share of our attention which is given to the influence of demand on value; and the longer the period, the more important will be the influence of cost of production

---

[3] Coase calls this blackboard economics. In his Nobel speech (Coase 1991) he said: "What is studied is a system which lives in the minds of economists but not on earth. I have called the result 'blackboard economics'. The firm and the market appear by name but they lack any substance. The firm in mainstream economic theory has often been described as a 'black box'. And so it is."

> on value. For the influence of changes in cost of production takes as a rule a longer time to work itself out than does the influence of changes in demand. The actual value at any time, the market value as it is often called, is often more influenced by passing events and by causes whose action is fitful and short lived, than by those which work persistently. But in long periods these fitful and irregular causes in large measure efface one another's influence; so that in the long run persistent causes dominate value completely. Even the most persistent causes are however liable to change. For the whole structure of production is modified, and the relative costs of production of different things are permanently altered, from one generation to another. (Ibid.: 349)

Substituting familiar texts with these earlier ways of discussing even what ought to be the most familiar of ideas plunges students into a new world that is on the one hand part of what they would be expected to understand – nothing about what Marshall wrote has been superseded – while on the other being strangely unfamiliar.

Using diagrams in the place of argument and reason changes the nature of economic instruction and tends to make such instruction more superficial. By teaching price determination as if it is merely about a meeting point between two lines when such lines have no existence and no one setting a price ever knows where they are or even thinks such concepts are of any direct relevance, we may be leaving students less capable of truly understanding the logic of economic adjustment.

Both micro and macro textbooks are saturated with diagrams that are seen as essential for an understanding of the conceptual framework being taught. Students who are compelled to explain such matters without diagrams but to use their economic logic instead are very different kinds of students and become better economists as well.

A similar argument could be made about the mathematisation of economics. A mathematical approach requires different kinds of thought processes and skills from an approach that focuses on theory and logic. Boulding's comment has been much repeated:

> The antihistorical school, which is now so common in the United States, where the history of thought is regarded as slightly depraved entertainment, fit only for people who really like medieval Latin, so that one became a fully-fledged, chartered Ph.D. economist without ever reading anything that was published more than ten years ago … leads to the development of slick technicians who know how to use computers,

> run massive correlations and regressions but who do not really know which side of anybody's bread is buttered, who are incredibly ignorant of economic institutions, who have no sense at all of the blood, sweat and tears that have gone into the making of economics and very little sense of any reality which lies beyond their data. (Boulding 1971: 232–3)

Fitting a trend line to a set of data is far different from understanding the dynamics of an economy in the process of change. To the extent that economics has become a science where logic has been replaced by manipulation of lines on a chart or statistical analyses of data sets without genuine insight, where there is a diminished stress on the underlying theory, then economics is the worse for it. The need for properly structured courses in the history of economic thought at the undergraduate level would meet an even stonier reception today than in the past yet may be more crucial than ever. Perhaps this is the next stage of physics envy. Physicists no longer have a theory that explains sub-atomic particles, only statistical guides to what will happen. But economies are not at the sub-atomic level. We do have theories to explain what goes on – as we always have. The proper education of an economist would ensure that economists would be almost as conversant with the economic theories of the past as they are with the theories which exist in the present.

5. Defending the history of economic thought

> Once again thanks for your support for the ERC which was absolutely decisive.
>
> (Professor Cristina Marcuzzo, former President of ESHET, in an email to the author following the decision by the European Research Council to keep the History of Economic Thought within its economics classification after the ERC had first decided on its exclusion)

The aim of this book is to explain the importance of the history of economic thought in the curriculum of economists. A book like this would not have had to be written if this were the consensus view amongst economists, but more importantly, it would not have had to be written if the continuation of HET within the study of economics were not under serious and on-going threat. The history of economic thought has two somewhat contradictory kinds of opposition. First of all, there are those mainstream economists who would like to end the challenge to the authority of textbook economics that HET allows to continue. And then there are those who themselves value HET but because it is not actively supported by the mainstream would like to see it become less of a challenge to the mainstream or even removed as a sub-discipline of economics and the study continued as part of the history of sciences in general. Although in most ways the two groups have little in common, the outcome they seek is largely the same.

There have been two major attempts to remove HET as an active component in the study of economics, one in Australia in 2007 and the second in Europe in 2011. Both failed, but only narrowly and at the eleventh hour. I was closely involved in both cases and it is those experiences that have motivated the writing of this book. Both episodes might have been related to particular moments in time, but that we will only know at some future date when all danger has passed. In the meantime this book is written to explain the role of the history of economics to the mainstream, but also to explain to historians of economics the kinds of steps they need to take in defending their subject.

A bit of personal history may be useful here. Most of my career has been spent as a lobbyist in Canberra, the Australian capital. I am therefore a latecomer to academic life but unlike most academics I have a long history in the dark arts of politics. And because of my work in Australia and my friendship with Professor Cristina Marcuzzo – which began when she was President of the European Society for the History of Economic Thought – I became closely involved in efforts that were being made first in Australia and then in Europe to remove the history of economic thought from within the economics classification. In Australia the agency involved was the Australian Bureau of Statistics (the ABS) whilst in Europe it was the European Research Council (the ERC).

Although political lobbying tends to have a bad name, it is one of the highest arts and crucial for the maintenance of civilised society. There are, of course, venal motives often associated with political decisions and major issues of self-interest. But the process of establishing disinterested bodies which can look at issues on behalf of the community as a whole is essential if anything is to be achieved. If we are to have both stability and orderly change such bodies are an absolute necessity.

It should also be quite clear that those who are part of decision-making bodies at the ABS or the ERC are individuals of the highest standing and personal integrity who undertake work in areas where decisions must be made. In making their decisions, especially in areas which for most members of such bodies are not part of their own expertise, they almost invariably welcome information and position papers that outline the concerns of the individual groups which will be affected by the decisions they make. But having said that, once a decision has been made it is extremely difficult to get that decision reversed. It is not quite a law of politics, but time is limited, no one wishes to revisit ground that has already been gone over, and usually whatever decision has been made has been the result of considerations that were sufficient in themselves. I therefore understood just how difficult it would be to reverse decisions that had already been made to remove HET from within the economics classification. In Australia's case we had two weeks to finalise our submissions to convince the ABS not to implement what they had already decided to do, and in Europe the final decision had already been made to remove HET in 2011 so efforts were directed towards having the subject restored in 2012 and thereafter. It is to the credit of both organisations that they were willing to reverse decisions which had already been made.

Looking at the global effects, had the re-classification gone ahead in Australia it would have affected only a few scholars although the knock-on potential would have been quite high. Had the same decision been made by the ERC, the effect would have been enormous and I suspect would have led to similar shifts elsewhere. There are international classification systems that are coordinated by international bodies. Changes in any of them tend to lead to similar changes in all.

Two points are being made here. The first is what a close run business the continuance of HET within the economics classification was. The decisions might well have been otherwise, an outcome which would have placed HET well beyond the study of economics and have made it all but unviable as an academic study by economists. This is a change that would have been far from benign.

Second, since these battles are far from over there has to be some understanding by those who wish to protect (and even expand) the study of HET of what they are up against and how to deal with these threats. This chapter is designed as a kind of template to help others to understand how to defend this crucial area of study from those who would see it removed as a sub-discipline of economics and therefore as a legitimate area of research and study by economists.

THE AUSTRALIAN CLASSIFICATION WARS OF 2007

During the middle months of 2007, the study of the history of economic thought within the Australian universities system found itself, along with economic history, in the midst of a battle for its very survival. On the surface it was no more than an administrative issue dealing with the classification of various academic disciplines and their constituent groupings. But because within this reclassification the aim was to relocate HET out of the economics discipline and into a catch-all social sciences grouping far removed from economics, the study of the history of economics in Australia was faced with almost immediate extinction.

It may sound like no more than a bit of housekeeping, and that was how these changes were presented, but in 2007 the Australian Bureau of Statistics (ABS) undertook a revision of its research classifications, in particular the Australian Standard Research Classification. The key proposal, to have been effective from 2008, was to remove from the Economics research classification the fields History of Economic Thought and Economic History. These two subjects were to be "relocated" into a new category labelled as "History, Archaeology, Religion and Philosophy" (HARP). It was also plainly indicated that this change was merely a half-way house, and that in any future revision History of Economic Thought and Economic History might be entirely eliminated.

The consequences of this reclassification would have been grim for anyone with a research interest in HET. Under the new classification, research in HET (and economic history) would no longer have been recognised as *economic* research by the ABS and other government departments. Rather all such studies would have been recorded as research activity within the new makeshift HARP grouping, very far indeed from the study of economics and economic theory.

In some sense it should not matter which category a piece of research might end up being placed within. But because universities and other government departments, including those bodies which fund academic research, do in fact pay close attention to the official research codes the result would have been the removal of the history of economic thought from economics departments, their natural home. Like everywhere else it is on the basis of publications that conference funding, promotion and, indeed, job opportunities depend. It would therefore have meant that HET scholars working in economics departments would either have had to change their research orientation to save themselves from retrenchment or attempt to transfer to parts of the university system where their research quantum would be both enumerated and valued.

But it was more than just the question of the relocation of a number of scholars that was at stake. Behind the classification superstructure lay an underlying disregard for the entire history of economic thought and economic history subject areas. The proposed research reclassifications had been exposed to peak academic bodies, the Australian Academy of Social Sciences and the Australian Academy of Humanities. Remarkably, the former had approved the revision of the research codes even though the academy had several eminent economic historians and historians of economics serving as Fellows.

Although there was evidence that the consultation process had been ineffective, with there having been problems in the transmission of the ABS proposal to the Fellows, the concern remained that those who ought to have been within the decision-making process were excluded. Indeed, it should be noted that the ABS argued that in making the revisions it was putting the Australian classification system into conformity with the new international standard. This was the *Frascati Manual*, which had been developed by the OECD to set out the classification groupings to be used by statistical agencies to gather R&D data. Our reading of the manual indicated that the ABS in Australia wrongly interpreted the manual in dealing with the history of economic thought and economic history, but that would have counted for little had the change been made.

In the end it was only by chance, and during a mere three-week period, that a major national and international effort was undertaken at the end of which the original decision was satisfactorily revised. The outcome was that HET is now to be classified as a subdiscipline within Economic Theory while economic history is to be included as part of Applied Economics.

REVERSING THE DECISION

This is how events unfolded. At the end of August 2007, an urgent note was sent out by John Lodewijk, the editor of the Australian journal, *History of Economics Review*, to let the entire History of Economic Thought Society of Australia (HETSA) membership know what the ABS had decided to do and that submissions were required by 12 September, that is, in less than three weeks. While others were trying to think through what ought to be done, because of my lobbying background I immediately put together the following plan of action which was adopted and put into effect over the subsequent three weeks.

1. The executive of the History of Economic Thought Society here in Australia needs to identify who the decision-makers are who have put this proposal forward, and more importantly, who will make the final decision to accept or reject this proposal. The executive needs to make contact with these people and seek a meeting between them and the HETSA executive.
2. There needs to be a group response put together by the HETSA executive that has the solid backing of the membership. Someone should take the responsibility to write this response and then circulate it to the rest of us for comment and ultimately for our support.
3. Each one of us who feels that they have something they can personally add to the collective arguments being drawn up by HETSA should do so. It would also be helpful but not necessary if these responses could be posted so that others could see what is being said and could add their support or provide additional perspectives in their own submissions.
4. There needs to be an international alert posted on the HES website to inform historians of economics around the world that there is a proposal to delete the History of Economic Thought and Economic History classifications as legitimate research fields in economics in Australia.
5. We should find out whether there is an Economic Historians Association in Australia. They should be contacted and we should make common cause with them.
6. We should also alert the Economics Society of Australia and ask for its assistance in maintaining these areas as recognisably important areas of research for economists. We should approach the head of every economic department in the public service to state their opposition to the reclassification of HET.
7. And certainly, with Ian Castles having been the former Chief Commonwealth Statistician, his support in approaching the ABS should be sought.
8. Those of us who have access to the media should attempt to have articles run on these issues.

Each and every one of these eight steps was taken and each was essential for the preservation of HET in Australia. While it may not be a template for future actions since each set of circumstances is different, some idea of the lengths which must be gone to is provided by this list. A letter from the president of the society is not enough nor are a few discussions and resolutions by the executive. Real lobbying is essential, which means putting together a well-argued case that is presented to the decision-making body so that those who are making the final decision have a proper understanding of the stakes involved. You cannot assume that those who are making the decision already understand what we know. *You must identify who is making the decision, find out and understand thoroughly the basis for the decision, explain in detail to those making the decision why that perspective may not be correct and then provide a better alternative.* The Australian example should be recognised as presenting a template for the kind of approach required.[1]

RATIONALES FOR THE RECLASSIFICATION

To a large extent, the problem for HET was that it was not seen as an essential element of the study of economics either within economics or outside. But in providing its rationales for the decisions taken, the ABS demonstrated that two issues were predominant.

The first basis for the reclassification related to research funding or R&D expenditures. It was argued that HET scholars rarely seek large amounts of public money to fund their research. The ABS was revising research classification for public policy purposes and as an accounting device. Basically, HET was not seen to be attracting enough public funding to bother with maintaining an entire line in their classification scheme. The ABS metric inherently contained no explicit valuation of the researchers' specialised and unique knowledge and expertise, acquired over a career-long involvement within

[1] The following discussion is adapted from papers put together after the ABS decision was made by the present author together with Alex Millmow, the HETSA President. See Kates and Millmow (2008a, 2008b and 2008c) for further elaboration on the Australian experience.

their discipline nor did it provide any evaluation of their insight, ingenuity and inventiveness.

In HET, as in other similar fields, academics can generate high quality research output without extensive research grants. Many HET scholars do not apply for research grants because the money they seek would be trifling compared with the sciences yet the application costs disproportionately high. While R&D grants are comparatively easy to quantify and compare there were other indicators of research such as, for instance, PhD completions and scholarly publications. By only considering R&D expenditures, an incomplete and misleading indicator of research activity was conveyed. Moreover, the use of R&D dollars by the ABS as a "measure" of importance indicated an alarming mindset in evaluating all non-directly "commercial" research. Although the social value of research is not measured by the amount of public funds expended, this was all the ABS had to go on. HET was therefore to be omitted because the totals were paltry in comparison with other fields even within the discipline of economics.

The second rationale for the relocation of HET into a minor, non-economics category was to assert that the history of economics did not employ the "processes" of economic theory but rather the processes it involved were primarily historical and philosophic. This was the sole issue raised that actually dealt with the nature of the history of economic thought as a subject area. The aim behind the relocation, according to the ABS, was to achieve "classification consistency with regards to the use of *processes* as the key driver of classification location" (italics added). Underpinning this was a judgement made at some level on what it is that economists do, and based on that judgement, some assessment of the techniques and processes used by such economists in undertaking their tasks.

In presenting this argument, it became evident that those behind the reclassification knew little about economics. Amongst economists it is clear enough that economics cannot be identified as a process but should be understood as a subject area. There are no specific processes that are universally used by economists to study economic issues, nor are there any processes common to any of the sciences that might not conceivably be adopted by economists. Economists use the widest variety of techniques to answer questions about the world. To try to identify an abstract approach to economic questions that delimits one's work as that of an economist is close to impossible.

The core question raised by the ABS was thus whether historians of economics are economists first and historians second, or are, instead, historians, or perhaps even philosophers, first and then economists second, assuming that they are even economists at all. The question was not whether one might have studied economic theory in undertaking one's research into some area in the history of economics, but whether even an economist in turning to HET is any longer either participating in the study and advancement of economic theory or involved in the application of economic processes and techniques in answering some economically relevant question.

MAJOR CONSIDERATIONS

In many ways, those who made the decision to relocate HET did so without very much serious reflection. It was largely an administrative procedure; more of an afterthought than a genuinely considered decision. It was seen by those who made the recommendation as little more than a tidying up exercise. But it is for that very reason that the issue is of such significance. If even our fellow social scientists on such decision-making bodies do not find such a relocation problematical, then the problem for historians of economics, and economic history, has reached a very high level indeed.[2]

The core issue raised was what exactly does it mean to be an economist. Without having thought much about it, virtually all HET specialists would have identified themselves as economists, as indeed would most of their colleagues. The tradition of teaching and learning in the history of economic theory had always been

[2] Here we might note that the actual process of consultation may have broken down, which in itself represents a problem of a different kind. Our researches into the procedures adopted indicated that within the social sciences review bodies involved, those who might have been expected to oppose the proposal to remove HET and EH from the economics classification, especially the historians of economics and the economic historians, did not seem to have been made aware of the proposed changes, a lesson in itself about what needs to be done to protect the future of both the history of economic thought and of economics itself.

undertaken by economists within schools of economics. The subject matter, aside from some largely biographical work on a few exceptionally well-known economists – especially amongst those whose work extends beyond the scope of traditional economic theory – was entirely within the province of schools of economics. Non-economists might have an interest in Adam Smith or John Stuart Mill for their work on moral or political philosophy, or be attracted to John Maynard Keynes because of his larger social role, but even then, interest in the more technical side of their economic work would have been almost entirely confined to economists.

The Australian Bureau of Statistics, in making its determination that historians of economics were not economists because they did not use the "processes" of economics, put the issue squarely on the table. What is it that makes one an economist and the work one does economics? Although the ABS did not specify just what it was that economists do, it was clear to it, and indeed to many others, that specialists in HET did not qualify.

But even if HET did manage to survive the initial threshold question as to whether specialists in the history of economics were in actual fact economists, the question really being raised was whether HET is for all that such a small and insignificant area that even if in some technical sense it is an area of economics and can be defended as such, it is one that nonetheless deserves no standing amongst the serious areas of economic theory and practice.

To put the issue at its starkest: no one specifically looks for an individual with expertise in the history of economic thought to answer any particular question in applied economics. From monetary policy to international trade, the skill set needed to devise policy is seldom seen to reside in individuals who have made the history of economic theory their specialist study. Yet as explained to the ABS, it is just such an expertise that is often amongst the most useful forms of knowledge for framing such policies, and that supplementing one's technical abilities with an understanding of the history of the theory in the relevant area deepens one's analytical skills and contributes to a more penetrating investigation of the topic under review.

WHAT ECONOMICS IS – WHAT ECONOMISTS DO

As far as the ABS was concerned, economics is not the allocation of scarce resources against a background of competing demands, nor is it a study of mankind in the ordinary business of life, nor is it an inquiry into the nature and causes of the wealth of nations. Economics is instead a series of technical approaches for handling particular sets of social questions that economists are asked to solve. The ABS sought a definition of economics that might provide an overview, as a statistical agency is wont to do, so that it could determine without a great deal of effort whether the specific work or research being undertaken fit into the parameters it had devised for its statistical classification scheme. It then made the sensible observation that when economists went about doing whatever it was they did, none of it involved looking at what economists one hundred years ago had been saying about the same subject. And in reaching this conclusion, the ABS could not have been more wrong.

In looking at these issues it should be borne in mind that economics is a policy science. Its role is not just to develop a set of abstract theoretical tools but is for the most part an attempt to provide a workable understanding of the nature and structure of the economy with the aim of framing economic policies. The vast majority of those with economics degrees will ultimately make their way in the world by applying the tools of the trade they learn in an attempt to resolve actual real-world social puzzles. It is therefore too narrow to explain the role of HET in terms of economics as an academic study, a broader view is needed in order to recognise explicitly the value of studying the history of economics as a means of learning and applying economic theory.

The issues discussed in defence of HET were grouped under a number of general headings, but all of these headings really had only a single purpose. They all attempted to demonstrate that a knowledge of the history of the relevant economic theories often provides added and useful depth to whatever theoretical or empirical studies are being made. The ideas that lie behind the following summaries were developed from the flood of submissions, both national and international, that descended upon the ABS when its original decision became known. It is these themes which have been expanded into the present volume.

One could not, of course, deny that it is possible to undertake an economic investigation without any knowledge whatsoever of the history of the relevant theory. It is clear enough that this is what occurs on a daily basis across the vast expanse of economics. It is also clear enough that there are trade-offs in time and effort involved in determining just which forms of knowledge one should gather and apply to the issue under review. But as explained, what should also be clear is that a better understanding of the history of the theory being studied or applied adds to the weight of useful knowledge available. In the original submission to the ABS, it was noted that the history of economic thought:

- is a pathway to understanding economic theory and its application
- provides a perspective on existing theory that provides orientation for its future development
- is a conversation with the economists of the past on contemporary questions
- is a storehouse of theoretical approaches for dealing with economic issues
- is a means of deepening one's understanding of contemporary theory
- provides a literary approach to dealing with economic issues different from but as valid as mathematical and statistical approaches
- is a means for training applied economists.[3]

None of this was to deny that studying the history of economics for the pure academic rewards that such knowledge provides is in itself often justification enough. There are indeed many such rewards and many who focus on HET do so for its own intrinsic interest. The study of the history of economic thought is valuable in its own right apart from any practical role it might play. But what was argued was that the study of the history of theory also provides a foundation for both economic research and applied economics, and that ignoring this role threatens to limit the value of economics and deplete the analytical ability of economists to handle the various

---

[3] Each of these bullet points has been discussed at greater length in Chapter 2.

questions they are asked to answer. Each of these issues was discussed only in brief. But the larger point, that an economist without a background in HET is less well equipped than one who does have such knowledge for dealing with straightforwardly economic questions, was the central contention of the submission made to the ABS.

The Australian experience ought to have been something of an alert to the entire international community of scholars within the history of economic thought. The growing disregard across the academic world for history of all kinds is well known, as is the still increasing role of mathematical approaches to economic issues. As a result, it went completely unnoticed outside the HET community when an administrative decision was taken which would for all practical purposes have been the death sentence in Australia for the study of both the history of economics and economic history. After an enormous effort, that decision turned out to be merely provisional and was ultimately overturned. But what had been made clear was that the decision to leave the two histories within the economics classification was itself merely provisional and would be reviewed each time the ABS looked to overhaul its classification scheme. It was therefore to remain an issue ever open for review.

It should not, however, be thought that either HET or EH were friendless and alone. From the Australian experience, it was evident that many amongst those in senior economic positions internationally and in Australia believed that HET (and EH) properly belonged within economics. But those at senior positions are typically those who took their degrees when HET was almost universally taught. As time goes by, this will be less and less the case. HET will henceforward need to show how and why it ought to hold its place in the side.

THE EUROPEAN EXPERIENCE 2011

The second episode was an almost identical attempted change in the classification system but this time in Europe. I was drawn in almost accidentally and as an afterthought only because I was at the time organising the HETSA conference in Melbourne and my special guest speaker was Cristina Marcuzzo, the former President of the European Society for the History of Economics (ESHET). As part of a letter to me in organising her visit to Australia she added the following. This was dated 19 February 2011.

> I am writing also about another matter. As you can see from the enclosed letter, we (HET people) are engaging a battle with EU to have HET included in the list of recognized field in the European Research Council (see ERC file). Would you – as HETSA – be willing to support our request, by writing to the Council members? I am enclosing the list with their e-mail address.
>
> Please let me know if Hetsa can help.
>
> With my best wishes,
> Cristina

Having been there once already, I was more than aware of how dangerous this situation was.

Original Letter Sent by ESHET Executive – 4 February 2011

This is the letter that had been sent to the ERC by the ESHET executive on 4 February 2011. It was addressed to the ERC President, Professor Helga Nowotny.

> Dear Professor Nowotny,
>
> It was brought to our attention that the ERC has decided to propose a classification system of economics which is comprised of 14 sub-areas. We note, with great dismay that the area of History of Economic Thought has been completely left out of this.
>
> We are the President and Secretary of the European Society for the History of Economic Thought (ESHET) – a society comprised of about 300 European academics – and we are concerned that such an omission represents only a very partial understanding of the intellectual dimension of economics as an academic discipline. We are also concerned that such a classification would deprive our members and all those who wish to research in the area of the History of Economics from proper access to research funding.
>
> The proposed classification seems almost to imply that economics is a discipline with an uncontested paradigmatic core and where most research and intellectual pursuits should be directed into the application of those agreed principles. More to the point, there is an implied presumption that a dialogue with facts and data is as straightforward as in some of the natural science. However, the reality is that as the subject matter of economic investigation is not indifferent to the way in

which we theorise about it, historical and cultural evolutions are not less significant to the understanding of the role of economics in society.

It is particularly interesting that at a time where organisations like the Institute for New Economic Thinking are calling for a return to the History of Economic Thought, the ERC chose to allow the distancing of the intellectual context of economics from its practitioners.

The History of Economic Thought is important for contemporary economics for two main reasons. Firstly, it may help understand the origin and significance of concepts which are currently taken for granted and presumed to have evolved from mere observations. Secondly, it may help enrich the way we think about economics. Unlike some of the natural sciences, the development of economic ideas has not always been based on the proper method of selecting a paradigm through testing. On many occasions, the directions economics took were influenced by less obvious reasons like, for instance, epistemology or the rise of mathematics. Consequently, the history of economics does not necessarily contain the foundations of modern thinking but also alternative ways for such thinking.

Many contemporary writers embellish their writing with quotes from the past. They do so because they themselves are not always quite sure what these concepts, like, for instance, the invisible hand, mean. On many occasions, the use of these quotes reflects more ignorance than support for the ideas expressed in the article.

A proper study of the past will enable to explore at all times the different alternatives which have been around to the thinking about society and the economy.

The self-confidence of economists in their theories has already led to the decline in job opportunities in the area of the History of Economics. Nevertheless, there is a thriving community of historians of economics. In addition to the European society which we represent, there are numerous national societies in Italy, France, Germany and the Nordic countries. There are annual gatherings in the UK and the Iberian Peninsula. There is also a thriving community in North America which is congregated around the History of Economics Society.

We would like to think that any Research Council will treat the landscape of researchers as it is rather than as someone would like it to be. Excluding the subject from research funding is an act which tampers with the landscape and may lead to the disappearance of an important aspect of the intellectual lives of all social scientists.

We would like to ask you to propose and support the adding of a 15th category called the History of Economics, Methodology and Institutions.

Yours Sincerely,

Professor Harald Hagemann	Professor Amos Witztum
President – ESHET	Secretary – ESHET

Letter from President of ERC Supporting Exclusion of HET – 17 March 2011

The ERC was not persuaded by the submissions it had received as the following note from the President of the ERC discusses. The decision outlined how research into the history of economic thought would be reclassified as "the study of the human past: archaeology, history and memory".

Dear Colleagues,

As I have received three letters from different associations regarding the lack of "history of economics" (or "history of economic thought") in the ERC's list of descriptors for the evaluation panel SH 1 ("Individuals, institutions and markets: economics, finance and management") in the last couple of weeks, I want to address you collectively. I want to thank all of you for your critical feedback. It is crucial for the ERC to stay in close contact with the academic community, in order to provide the right kind of opportunities for your research.

Regarding your concerns let me first clarify one crucial point: Unlike your impression, the ERC panel descriptors do not form a classification. Rather, their main and only purpose is to provide information to applicants which panel to apply to. This is a very sensitive issue, and hence the distinction is important. The ERC is open to every kind of bottom-up frontier research, based on every theoretical or empirical approach. Panels are multi-disciplinary by definition, with very broad expertise, in order to cover all fields.

Of course, there is a tendency to mainstream sciences, which may be even stronger in the social sciences. But we do not think that this affects the ERC, as can be shown by the projects that have and continue to be funded. Addressing your concern, "history of economics" is divided between SH1 and SH6 ("The study of the human past: archaeology, history and memory"). The decision which panel assesses which project proposal is done primarily by the applicant. Panel Chairs may re-assign projects if they feel that a given project falls outside the expertise of the members of their panel and if the panel chair of the other panel agrees to include it.

I hope this clarifies the issue and also helps to eliminate your concerns.

With best regards,
Helga Nowotny

MY LETTER IN RESPONSE TO THE ORIGINAL ERC DECISION – 21 MARCH 2011

Importantly, the letter from the ERC clearly outlined their criteria for judgement and their concerns. The way these issues were viewed was not how these matters were viewed by those of us who dealt with HET. I therefore drafted a reply to the ERC – there would have been others, of course – in which the aim was to explain how the Council's understanding of the relevant issues was not in accordance with our understanding.

Dear Professor Nowotny

Thank you for your letter which has helped to clarify the issues. The need for clarity is important since I believe there has not been sufficient appreciation of the nature of the concerns that have been raised. Unfortunately, the proposed changes constitute much more than just a slight alteration in the classification system. The underlying reality behind the ERC proposal is that it will profoundly change the nature of the study of economics for the worse. I should note here that I am writing to you and to the ERC on my own behalf, but as I am in the midst of writing a book on these very issues [this book] I feel I can claim a specialist expertise.

In your letter, you wrote:

> Regarding your concerns let me first clarify one crucial point: Unlike your impression, the ERC panel descriptors do not form a classification. Rather, their main and only purpose is to provide information to applicants which panel to apply to. This is a very sensitive issue, and hence the distinction is important. The ERC is open to every kind of bottom-up frontier research, based on every theoretical or empirical approach. Panels are multi-disciplinary by definition, with very broad expertise, in order to cover all fields.

In my view this misses the crucial point. Whatever the ERC may believe about what is the "main and only purpose" of the panel descriptors, that is not the only purpose that others will use this classification system for. It will now be used to define what is and what is not an element of the study of economics.

Let me use my own personal circumstances as an example of why this misreads the problem. I have written extensively on the "Keynesian Revolution". In 1936, Keynes published his *General Theory of Employment, Interest and Money* which almost immediately became the standard framework for the discussion of macroeconomic issues as it remains today. The stimulus packages that were introduced following the Global Financial Crisis were universally and correctly described as Keynesian.

As I am critical of the consequences of the Keynesian Revolution, much of my work has required a return to an examination and discussion of the economics that preceded the advent of Keynesian economics. The question that is now before the ERC is whether my work should be seen as part of economics or as part of the study of something else. That is, to which panel would I apply to seek funds to continue my research?

If my research is classified as history, then my university department will no longer consider my work economics and will no longer allow me to undertake such studies. It further means that no one interested in pursuing a career as an economist would even consider work in this area.

The fact of the matter is that even though this part of the study of economic theory is described as the "history" of economics, it is not history as such. These are in depth studies into economic theory. Such studies can and do influence the future direction of the discipline whether or not that is the actual intent of those who have undertaken the research. It makes no difference what the actual purpose behind any individual study may be, the effect of examining the history of economic thought will affect, however marginally and incrementally in any particular instance, the way economic issues are discussed.

And the fact is that historians of economics, who are almost universally economists, are doing work as economists in looking at the history of their subject. To suggest that there will be some multi-disciplinarian panel to which economists studying the history of their subject may apply for funding somewhere out beyond economics itself means that they must apply for funding in competition with scholars who are actually studying history.

But the issue of funding is far from being the most significant. The ERC "panel descriptors" are making a statement about where to locate the history of economic thought in amongst all of the forms of study that are currently identified. These panel descriptors constitute a classification system. They are a sorting mechanism. If they were not a form of classification, it should be a matter of indifference to the ERC where the history of economics is included and there would be no effort made to exclude history of economics from the economics classification.

In framing this classification system, there needs to be some appreciation of the difference between the natural sciences and the social sciences. Theories in the natural science are validated largely through experimental work. Theoretical beliefs are tested against a background reality to determine whether in a controlled environment the theoretical beliefs can withstand empirical investigation. If a theory is valid then we should see some particular outcome from a properly designed experiment. The essence of proof within the natural sciences is found in the conduct of repeatable experiments.

In the social sciences there are seldom if ever repeatable experiments of consequence. The social sciences are almost entirely validated through the collective opinion of the members of the profession. There is a vast number of members in every social science and the mainstream is forged through an agreement amongst the members of the profession on what a correct answer to some question is. There are no radical experiments of the Morley-Michelson variety in the social sciences that can send the profession in search of new answers.

The closest we have had in recent times to an experiment in economics has taken place through the stimulus packages that were introduced following the Global Financial Crisis. Given the profusion of other factors that have affected economic outcomes in each of these economies, there can have been no decisive demonstration one way or the other of the effect that these policies have had. It is precisely here that the history of economic thought has a role to play, and the role it plays is part of economic theory and not history.

You further wrote:

> "Of course, there is a tendency to mainstream sciences, which may be even stronger in the social sciences. But we do not think that this affects the ERC, as can be shown by the projects that have and continue to be funded. Addressing your concern, 'history of economics' is divided between SH1 and SH6 ('The study of the human past: archaeology, history and memory'). The decision which panel assesses which project proposal is done primarily by the applicant. Panel Chairs may re-assign projects if they feel that a given project falls outside the expertise of the members of their panel and if the panel chair of the other panel agrees to include it."

For someone with an understanding of the role of the history of economics within economic theory, "the study of the human past: archaeology, history and memory" is completely inadequate as a description of what the history of economics actually does. The history of economics looks at the development of economic theory, the different roads it took, the various debates that occurred, the different conclusions that were reached at different times. Most importantly, it is a storehouse of ideas that far from being only of historic interest serving merely as a prelude to the present, they are in fact alternative ways of looking at economic events that may have relevance now or at some stage in the future. Historians of economics provide an in-depth understanding of the conclusions reached by economists at an earlier period. Without the work done by such historians of economics, no economist in the present would have ready access to the views of economists of the past.

What these historians of economics do is examine previous theoretical models so that even while they are looking at these theories they have at the back of their minds, if not actually in the foreground, the economic issues of their own times. It is not possible, for example, to look at the work of Adam Smith, Karl Marx, Ludwig von Mises or John Maynard Keynes without drawing insights into the economic circumstances of one's own time. This is the actual relevance of the history of economics to economics.

That is why we wrote to you to say that it is with considerable alarm we view the provisional decision by the European Research Council not to include the history of economic thought in its list of sub-categories within economics. Since the study of the history of economics is already an established part of economics, as it has been from its very earliest days, this decision appears to ignore the actual existing practice of economics and seems to be an attempt to change the nature of the subject itself. Why the ERC should feel that it should take such an approach is difficult to understand.

We here in Australia found ourselves in the same circumstances in 2007. Our Bureau of Statistics had made a provisional decision to exclude both History of Economic Thought and Economic History from within the economics classification. The word "history" had led some to the conclusion that these are not proper areas in the study of economics but are forms of history and are therefore part of the humanities and not an integral component of economics itself. We here in Australia therefore went to a considerable effort to demonstrate that both HET and EH are not just a component of economics but a necessary component. Both are absolutely essential for the study of economics, and without these components economic theory is less capable of undertaking its intended research.

Economics is a social science and a policy science. It is, as already noted, not a natural science. With the natural sciences, the history of the development of the theory is just that, history. While it might have some uses for a scientist in learning the processes of the scientific method itself, the theories themselves are certainly only of historical interest. No discarded scientific theory is ever resurrected except in very unusual circumstances and in a vastly different form.

Economics is different. The most significant revolution in economic theory during the twentieth century occurred because John Maynard Keynes was reading the works of Thomas Robert Malthus which had been written more than a century before. The Malthusian approach to demand deficiency is, of course, vastly different from the Keynesian but the aim and intent of both was the same. We are now in an analogous position where economic theory has again shown that it may not be up to the task at hand. There are therefore efforts being made to look at other approaches to thinking about economic issues, and many of these are attempts to look at the theories of the past.

One can understand how those who believe that the current set of established theories ought to be left alone and untroubled by historical comparisons with previous ways of looking at things and would feel pleased by the decision to exclude an examination of the history or economic thought. Both HET and EH have the effect of putting existing ways of looking at economic issues under the microscope. At this very moment, the economic problems confronting us across the world may to a significant extent be due to the faulty economic theories that have been used to frame policy. Alternative ways of thinking about such issues is unlikely to be found in some novel idea never before considered but in looking again at different theoretical possibilities that are found within the history of the subject.

Similarly, the use of economic techniques to look back at historical episodes is one of the few ways in which economic theories can be tested. There are no laboratory experiments in economics. We only have our historical experience that can be used to validate the theories we apply.

I will, lastly, note that it is only the mainstream of the economics profession that holds this attitude to the study of the history of economic thought. All other schools of thought consider their own history as extremely important, irrespective of whether one holds a strongly free market approach or instead seeks ever greater centralised control over economic outcomes.

On the one side, there are the Austrian economists who hold in great esteem their own historic predecessors, economists such as Weser, Menger, Bohm-Bowerk, Mises or Hayek. No one studying Austrian economics fails to be made acquainted with the works of these writers as well as many others. On the other side, there are Marxist economists who begin their understanding of economic issues through the works of Karl Marx and Friedrich Engels. Beyond that great authors in this tradition would include Kautsky, Luxemburg, Mandel, Sweezey and Barun. Indeed, every single school of economic thought, other than the mainstream, consciously learns from its predecessors.

Because of our experience dealing with the attempt by our Bureau of Statistics to remove the History of Economic Thought from the Economics classification, I am in the midst of completing a book on the crucial role of HET as part of economics. The book is to be titled, *Defending the History of Economic Thought*. HET cannot be separated from economics without creating almost fatal damage to the study of the history of economics. But more importantly, as the book tries to show, economics cannot be separated from HET without suffering immense damage to the ability of economic theory to renew itself in the face of new circumstances and problems.

I therefore attach for your interest a copy of the still incomplete introduction to the book that discusses some of these issues [which now in an expanded form constitutes Chapter 2 of this volume]. The remainder of the book will discuss the crucial significance of HET for economic theory.

I will also attach a paper that has been included in a book just published at the end of last year, *The First Great Recession of the 21st Century: Competing Explanations*. The main title of my article (Kates 2011) was, "The History of Economic Thought and Public Policy", and deals with the crucial role that HET plays in renewing economic thought.

It is a major concern for myself, the community of historians of economics but also for every economist working outside the mainstream tradition as well as for many who work within the mainstream, that the ERC would be contemplating excluding the history of economic thought from what is otherwise such a comprehensive list of sub-disciplines within economics. The Australian Bureau of Statistics, when it made its final decision on its classifications included the History of Economic Thought as part of Economic Theory and Economic History as part of Applied Economics.

It seems to me that a similar outcome would be available to the ERC. The inclusion of an additional category dealing with History of Economic Thought and Economic History would not compromise the integrity of the classification system. Alternatively these areas could put these into one of the other categories, such as SH1_2, "Development, economic growth". There seems to be no reason to actively exclude what has been traditionally such an important area of economic thinking from part of what ought to be a comprehensive and properly structured classification system.

Merely because the word "history" appears in the traditional name of the subject is neither a profound nor a satisfactory reason for shifting the history of economics into a descriptor entirely remote from the study of economics. Rather than being properly precise, it is the reverse. It is grouping the history of economic thought with subject areas with which it has almost nothing in common other than the name. Historians of economics do not study history, they study economics. This is the crucial distinction that needs to be made by the European Research Council in devising its classification system.

Your sincerely
Dr Steven Kates

Letter by President of ERC Reversing Original Decision – 28 April 2011

The following letter, dated 28 April 2011, was sent out by Professor Nowotny, the President of the ERC, announcing the Council's decision to re-include the history of economic thought within its classification system from 2012 onwards. How significant my own letter was in the final decision is an unknown, but as Professor Marcuzzo noted in an email to me, "once again thanks for your support for the ERC which was absolutely decisive." Whatever may have been the precise reason for the change, the decision to maintain the history of economic thought within the economics classification was the result.

> Dear colleagues,
>
> Many thanks for raising your concerns regarding the inclusion of history of economic thought and economic history. The ERC's Scientific Council understands its own role to serve the academic community and therefore we take your remarks very seriously.
>
> I can inform you that first steps were taken to make HET (history of economic thought) and EH (economic history) more visible in the guide for applicants. As the Calls for 2011 have already been published, the change can take effect only from 2012 on. Descriptor SH1_14 of the SH1 panel (Individuals, institutions and markets: economics, finance and management) will be changed to
>
> > "History of economics and economic thought, quantitative and institutional economic history".
>
> Please note that formally this adjustment still has to be confirmed by the Committee on Panels and adopted by the ERC Scientific Council. Personally, I see no resistance to the proposed change in descriptors. I would also like to reiterate that the main function of the descriptor is to provide guidance for the applicants in whose responsibility it will also lie in the future where to apply.
>
> Once again, let me thank you for sharing your concerns and your contributions.
>
> With kind regards,
> Helga Nowotny

LEARNING FROM THE HISTORY OF THE HISTORY OF ECONOMICS

This was an enlightened and sensible decision and the right decision. It recognised the importance of the history of economics as part of economics itself. The President and the Council cannot be praised enough because, rather than being defensive about their original decision and digging in as others might have done, they understood the weight of the argument and reversed their original course.

Although the history of these events is important, the main reason for describing their sequence is to emphasise the kinds of actions that are necessary to deal with attempts to remove the history of economics as an economics sub-discipline. There are others who would like to do so and there are means at their disposal to effect that outcome. It is important to learn from these near calamities if HET is to be preserved as an important area of study amongst economists.

A Partial Programme

This book, and this chapter in particular, is about preserving the role of HET. But it is also about expanding the role of HET, to make others understand its importance in the education of a sound economist and in the improvement of economics as a policy science. It's not enough to be forming a circle of the wagons to fight off the various attempts to remove the history of economics from economics. There needs to be a further effort made to extend the role of HET and this can only be done if that role is explained by historians of economics and understood by a wider circle of economists.

And let's face it, economists who have not studied the history of their subject are going to be reluctant to involve themselves in something they have no familiarity with. They have little reason to expect any professional dividend from an examination of the economic theory of the past. It is perfectly obvious that if no one studies the history of economics then no one is better off than anyone else. And it is also perfectly obvious that entire careers can be built, honours received, Nobel Prizes won without ever having even so much as glanced at the works of any economist other than those of their contemporaries. It is simply not evident to the majority of economists that there is anything missing in their own education or the education of their students. And if no one rocks the boat by bringing the history of economics into the mainstream conversation, this condition can go on endlessly without change.

I therefore offer this 12-step programme to advance the history of economic thought amongst economists. These are just my own considered thoughts and are neither definitive nor exhaustive. They are provided merely as an initial set of suggestions that hopefully others will adopt, expand on and seek to implement.

First, clarify and explain what an economist should be familiar with from the history of economics and why it will make a difference to them in their professional lives. Economics has an exciting past that has been at the centre of political controversy since its earliest days. The Cold War when reduced to its essence was about how to manage an economy for the greatest benefit of the greatest number. Political debate to this day revolves around economic issues. Not all that much has changed. There is plenty to learn from the past. Historians of economics should help clarify and explain the ways in which studying HET can contribute to making an economist a better economist.

Second, there needs to be more engagement between HET and mainstream issues. The attitude of many historians of economics who look after our journals is that there ought to be no matters of contemporary policy relevance included. In their view, journals devoted to the history of economics should be restricted to looking at the historical record in the development of theory. No space should be given to policy issues or theoretical considerations that are built on past theories. The wall of separation between HET and the mainstream should instead be broken down. HET journals should start contesting in the area of modern theoretical development.

Third, build alliances with the mainstream of the profession. Most economists would be interested in possessing a greater knowledge of the history of economics if it were easier to acquire than it is. It is not hard to convince most economists that there is value in knowing more of what previous economists had written. There is only a reluctance to believe that the effort and time required to acquire this knowledge will have any net return. More effort should be made to interest the mainstream in HET.

Fourth, major historians of economics should attempt to have articles published in major theoretical journals. Articles dealing with the history of economics should become a feature of the economics journals and the editors of such journals should see part of their role as trying to find articles on the history of economics that fit within the scope of their own conception of what the journal is designed to cover. There was a time in the past when HET articles were commonly found in economics journals in general. HET is not specialist in the way, say, monetary theory is. The history of economics deals with all of the economic fields and should therefore have a presence within every economic journal.

Fifth, papers on the history of economics given at mainstream conferences should not be hived off to some HET section for historians of economics to discuss amongst themselves but should be included where they thematically belong. Sessions on monetary theory, for example, could and should include papers based on theoretical, statistical and historical analyses. The economics of the past has light to shed on contemporary issues.

Sixth, at least some historians of economics should craft their papers, where appropriate, so that the contemporary relevance of the issues discussed are highlighted. A number of historians of economics do that already. The aim would be to encourage the acceptance within the mainstream of such papers. Conferences with refereed papers should have no concerns about such a procedure nor should historians of economics. If historical material has relevance in the conversation today, it is a mistake to exclude such contributions.

Seventh, historians of economics should take the trouble to make the case that the study of HET makes an economist a better economist. That is what this book is for and I am hardly the last person alive to think it. The case is often made within specialist HET journals but there is little point in preaching to the converted. We make PhD students do the literature search for a reason and we insist that they know the entire thread of the previous development in whatever area of theory they are dealing with. We therefore acknowledge the importance of the historical background and the need to have understood both sides of the issues investigated.

Eighth, it should become a matter of personal concern to any economist to find themselves unaware in detail of the historical developments that led to the theories they use entering the mainstream. We make a vague pass at discussing the "Keynesian revolution" or the "marginal revolution". Most texts provide thumbnail portraits of economists of the past with some discussion of their contributions. We therefore collectively appreciate that there is value in this knowledge. We only fail to institutionalise this understanding within the curricula we devise.

Ninth, early warning sensory devices need to be put in place within decision-making structures that can affect the position of the history of economic thought. It has to be understood by historians of economics that HET has no home if it is not part of economics itself. There may be some sense that historians are receiving the cold shoulder and that there are other homes we can go to if we are not wanted amongst the economics community. Do not be deceived. Only economists can do the history of economics properly and economics is a lesser subject, less penetrating and less worthy, if its history is removed from its official field of study. Economists in general should demand its continuance amongst economists, and most would do so if they understood there were even such threats around. But it can be, and it will only be, historians of economics who will be sensitive to these dangers and it is their responsibility, through their executive organisations who enlist their membership's contacts and goodwill, to defend HET when it is under threat. No one else can do it and no one else will.

Tenth, threats by decision-making bodies to the continuance of the history of economics should be treated as a three-alarm fire. Nothing should be held back. Such threats should be treated with complete seriousness because you may be sure that if such issues have been raised at all there is an actual agenda behind it. It will either be someone who wishes to tidy up a classification system or someone who may harbour ill will towards the future continuance of HET. But whatever the motivation of those proposing the change, there should be no doubt that dealing with such actions requires serious effort. Nothing is ever "irreversible" but if HET should ever fall outside of the economics category it will put a very large damper on its future progress. Do not let it happen. Look at the list of actions that were taken in Australia in 2007. It took all of that to reverse a decision that should never have been made in the first place. Those are the kinds of actions that should be adopted if it does appear that such a threat has materialised. It is better to demonstrate that you are prepared for a fight than to find HET disappear because no one was prepared to make the effort to preserve it.

Eleventh, you should think through what actions will succeed in expanding knowledge of the history of economics. The proposal advanced in this book is to suggest that economists spend at least a semester as part of their studies in reading the textbooks of much earlier times and then discovering the reasons why those textbooks had changed. Nothing written in the twentieth century is so archaic so as to have become inaccessible to any student who can read an introductory text today. It is not the style of writing that will be unfamiliar but the conceptual background. And while most texts written in the nineteenth century will be harder to follow, just as reading Dickens is harder to follow, there is nothing that ought to be impassable in Jevons, Marshall or any of their contemporaries.

Twelfth, make the extension of the history of economics part of your own personal mission statement even if it is well down the list of your priorities. Anyone with an interest in any part of the history of economics will have experienced others discussing some matter that can be illuminated by their own knowledge from economic theory's past. It should become an objective for historians of economics to bring HET themes into discussions of contemporary issues as a reminder that there are ideas, theories and concepts from the earlier days of economic theory that actually are relevant even today.

Bibliography

Akerlof, George (2007), "The Missing Motivation in Macroeconomics", *American Economic Review*, **97** (March 2007), 3–36.

Bagehot, Walter ([1873] 1915), *Lombard Street: A Description of the Money Market*, new edition with an introduction by Hartley Withers, London: Smith, Elder and Co.

Baumol, William J. (1988), *Economics: Principles and Policy*, Orlando, FL: Harcourt Brace Jovanovich.

Becker, Gary and William J. Baumol (1952), "The Classical Economic Theory: The Outcome of the Discussion", *Economica*, **19**, 355–76.

Blaug, Mark (1968), *Economic Theory in Retrospect*, revised edn, Homewood, IL: Richard D. Irwin, Inc.

Blaug, Mark (2001), "No Ideas Please, We're Economists", *Journal of Economic Perspectives*, **15** (1), 145–64.

Boulding, Kenneth (1971), "After Samuelson, Who Needs Adam Smith?", *History of Political Economy*, **3** (2), 225–37.

Bowmaker, Simon (2012), "Interview with E. Roy Weintraub (Duke University)", *The Art and Practice of Economics Research: Lessons from Leading Minds*, Cheltenham, UK and Northampton, MA, USA: Edward Elgar. Online at http://public.econ.duke.edu/~erw/erw.homepage_files/Simon%20Bowmaker%20interview.pdf (accessed 19 February 2013).

Chamberlain, E. ([1933] 1965), *The Theory of Monopolistic Competition: A Re-orientation of the Theory of Value*, 8th edn, Boston, MA: Harvard University Press.

Cliffe Leslie, T.E. (1888), "The Political Economy of Adam Smith", in *Essays in Political Economy*, 2nd edn, Dublin: Hodges, Figgis, & Co.

Coase, Ronald (1991), Nobel Prize Lecture. Online at http://www.nobelprize.org/nobel_prizes/economics/laureates/1991/coase-lecture.html (accessed 19 February 2013).

Froman, Lewis A. (1940), *Principles of Economics*, with the editorial assistance of Harlan L. McCracken, Chicago: Richard D. Irwin Inc.

Haberler, Gottfried von (1937), *Prosperity and Depression: A Theoretical Analysis of Cyclical Movements*, Geneva: League of Nations.

Jevons, William Stanley ([1871] 1888), *The Theory of Political Economy*, 3rd edn, London: Macmillan.

Kates, Steven (2010), "Influencing Keynes: The Intellectual Origins of the General Theory", *History of Economic Ideas*, **XVIII** (3), 33–64.

Kates, Steven (2011), 'The Role of the History of Economic Thought in the Development of Economic Theory and Policy", in Óscar Dejuán, Eladio Febrero and Maria Cristina Marcuzzo (eds), *The First Great Recession of the 21st Century: Competing Explanations*, Cheltenham, UK and Northampton, MA, USA: Edward Elgar, pp. 160–70.

Kates, Steven and Alex Millmow (2008a), "The History Wars of Economics: The Classification Struggle in the History of Economic Thought", *History of Economics Review*, **47**, 110–24.

Kates, Steven and Alex Millmow (2008b), "A Canary in the Coalmine: The Near Death Experience of History of Economics in Australia", *History of Economic Ideas*, **XVI** (3), 79–94.

Kates, Steven and Alex Millmow (2008c), "A Canary in the Coalmine: A Rejoinder", *History of Economic Ideas*, **XVI** (3), 112–18.

Keynes, John Maynard (1925), "Alfred Marshall, 1842–1924", in A.C. Pigou (ed.), *Memorials of Alfred Marshall*, London: Macmillan, p. 12.

Keynes, John Maynard ([1936] 1973), *The General Theory of Employment, Interest and Money*, London: Macmillan.

Mankiw, N. Gregory (2007), *Principles of Economics*, 4th edn, Mason, OH: Thompson Higher Education.

Manuel, Frank E. (1962), *The Prophets of Paris: Turgot, Condorcet, Saint-Simon, Fourier, Comte*, New York: Harper & Row.

Marshall, Alfred ([1920] 1947), *Principles of Economics: An Introductory Volume*, 8th edn, London: Macmillan and Co. Limited.

McCloskey, Deirdre (1986), "Economics as an Historical Science", in W.N. Parker (ed.), *Economic History and the Modern Economist*, Oxford: Blackwell, pp. 63–9.

McConnell, Campbell (1960), *Economics: Principles, Problems, and Policies*, 1st edn, New York: McGraw-Hill.

McCulloch, John Ramsay ([1825] 2011), *The Principles of Political Economy: With Some Enquiries Respecting their Application, and a Sketch of the Rise and Progress of the Science*, Whitefish, MT: Kessinger Publishing.

Mill, John Stuart ([1871] 1921), *Principles of Political Economy with Some of their Applications to Social Philosophy*, 7th edn, edited with an introduction by Sir W.J. Ashley, London: Longmans, Green, and Co.

Mill, John Stuart ([1874] 1974), "Of the Influence of Consumption on Production", in *Essays on Some Unsettled Questions of Political Economy*, 2nd edn, Clifton, NJ: Augustus M. Kelley, pp. 47–74.

Robinson, Joan (1933), *The Economics of Imperfect Competition*, London: Macmillan & Co.

Samuelson, Paul ([1948] 2012), *Economics: The Original 1948 Edition*, New York: McGraw-Hill.

Schabas, Margaret (1992), "Breaking Away: History of Economics as History of Science", *History of Political Economy*, **24**, 187–203.

Smith, Adam ([1776] 1976), *An Inquiry into the Nature and Causes of the Wealth of Nations*, edited by Edwin Cannan, Chicago: University of Chicago Press.

Taussig, F.W. ([1911] 1932), *Principles of Economics*, 3rd edn, New York: Macmillan.

Taylor, Fred M. ([1913] 2008), *Principles of Economics*, 2nd edn, Whitefish, MT: Kessinger Publishing's Rare Reprints.

Taylor, Fred M. (1925), *Principles of Economics*, 9th edn, New York: The Ronald Press Company.

Taylor, Fred M. (1929), "The Guidance of Production in a Socialist State", *American Economic Review*, **19** (1), 1–8, reprinted in *On the Economic Theory of Socialism* (1938) and *Socialism and the Market: The Socialist Calculation Debate Revisited* (2000).

Weintraub, E. Roy (2002), "Will Economics Ever have a Past Again?", *History of Political Economy*, **34** (supp. 1), 1–14.

Weintraub, E. Roy (2007), "Economic Science Wars", *Journal of the History of Economic Thought*, **29** (3), 1–14.

Society for the History of Economics (SHOE) Postings [Chapter 3]

The entire correspondence can be viewed at: https://listserv.yorku.ca/cgi-bin/wa?A1=ind0903d&L=shoe for weeks 2, 3 and 4 of March 2009

The specific postings discussed in this chapter are found at the following addresses within the SHOE archive:

First Steve Kates posting:
https://listserv.yorku.ca/cgi-bin/wa?A2=ind0903b&L=shoe&T=0&P=1127

First Roy Weintraub posting:
https://listserv.yorku.ca/cgi-bin/wa?A2=ind0903d&L=shoe&T=0&P=2531

Second Steve Kates posting in reply to Roy Weintraub:
https://listserv.yorku.ca/cgi-bin/wa?A2=ind0903d&L=shoe&T=0&P=2911

Steve Medema posting:
https://listserv.yorku.ca/cgi-bin/wa?A2=ind0903d&L=shoe&T=0&P=4125

Third Steve Kates posting in reply to Steve Medema:
https://listserv.yorku.ca/cgi-bin/wa?A2=ind0903d&L=shoe&T=0&P=5238

Second Roy Weintraub posting:
https://listserv.yorku.ca/cgi-bin/wa?A2=ind0903d&L=shoe&T=0&P=5997

Fourth Steve Kates posting in reply to Roy Weintraub's second posting:
https://listserv.yorku.ca/cgi-bin/wa?A2=ind0903e&L=shoe&T=0&P=659

Index